Ours is essentially a tragic age, so we refuse to take it tragically. The cataclysm has happened, we are among the ruins, we start to build up new little habitats, to have new little hopes. It is rather hard work: there is now no smooth road into the future: but we go round, or rather scramble over the obstacles. We've got to live, no matter how many skies have fallen.

D.H. LAWRENCE
from *Lady Chatterley's Lover*

Published by Little Toller Books in 2021

Photography: pg 8, 84, 122 by kind permission of Martyn Thomas, pages 13, 30, 90, 112, 117, 120 by kind permission of the family of the late Joanna Dunn, pg 58/59, 94, 103 by kind permission of Katherine Weaver, pg 74 by kind permission of John Barrett, pg 44, 147, 150 © Larraine & Ken Worpole

Maps: pg 6 © Ian Worpole

Typeset in Garamond by Little Toller Books

Printed in Cornwall by TJ Books

All papers used by Little Toller Books are natural, recyclable products made from wood grown in sustainable, well-managed forests

A catalogue record for this book is available from the British Library

ISBN 978-1-908213-86-0

No Matter How Many Skies Have Fallen

Back to the land in wartime Britain

Ken Worpole

Ken Worpole

LITTLE TOLLER

For Larraine, Ben, Anna, Andy,
Joe and Ruby, always and for ever

Contents

FRATING HALL FARM
Essex
Historic Field System
Circa 1950
Blue Barn
Colchester 7
Clacton 9
Hill House
Frating Green
King's Arms (P.H.)
Holly Farm
Camp Field
Gravel Pit Field
Swingate & Long
Frating Lodge
Mannings
Fratinghall Wood
Great Mill Field
Ram Field
Birch Field
The Twenty-Seven Acre
Horse Meadow
Brakey Field
Captain's Field
Acres Cottage Field
Frating Hall
Great Barn
The Sack Loft
Gt. Birchards Field
Horells
Captain's Wood
The Twenty Acres
Church Field
Church
Middle Field
Drive Field
Alresford Bottoms
Rates Field
Slough House
FRATING
Rectory
Barr's Farm

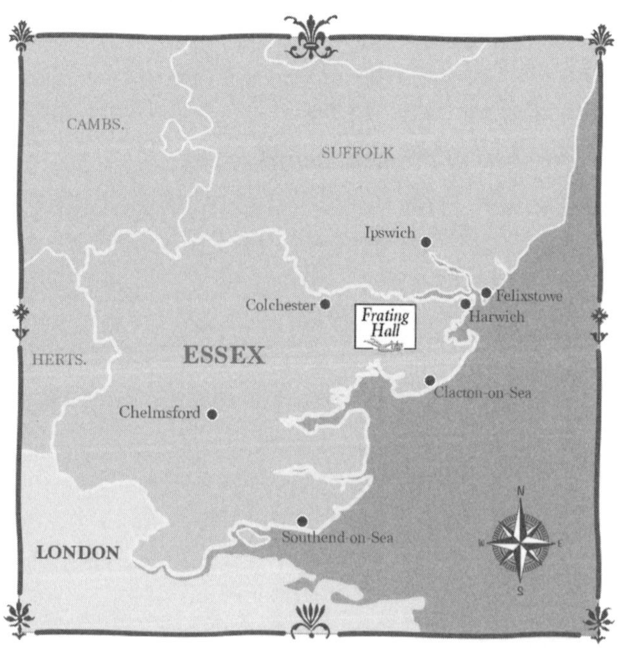
CAMBS.
SUFFOLK
Ipswich
Felixstowe
Colchester
Frating Hall
Harwich
HERTS.
ESSEX
Clacton-on-Sea
Chelmsford
Southend-on-Sea
LONDON
N
S

Introduction

'Simone Weil believed that the way to write was to pay attention. One should think of oneself, she said, as the careful and meticulous translator, and not the originator, of the ideas to be expressed.'

RICHARD REES ON SIMONE WEIL, 1958

In 2019 I gave a talk at the Firstsite Gallery in Colchester as part of the Essex Book Festival. It was based on an essay I had written the previous year on alternative communities for a book called *Radical Essex*. That book came out of an exhibition organised by the Focal Point Gallery in Southend, in which artefacts, photographs, models, films and audio-recordings captured the extensive tradition of radical social movements in the county in the twentieth century. These included Russian anarchist outposts on the Dengie Peninsula, the arrival of British naturism at Wickford, model industrial settlements and early modernist architecture at East Tilbury and Silver End, pioneering agricultural smallholdings at Ardleigh and Maylandsea, the social gospel tradition at Thaxted, trade union and women workers' militancy at Dagenham, religious and therapeutic retreats on Osea Island, at Bradwell and Stock, and much else. It was an exhibition that challenged the idea that Essex was a county with little history of interest to speak of, bereft of ideas or imagination. In reality, Essex, in its pre-1965 territorial and administrative boundaries and ever since, has

Frating Hall Farm Yard, circa 1948. To the left, Frating Hall, the single-storey brick building in the centre, is the workshop block, behind which was a second workshop, now demolished. A corner of the clapboard barn can be seen on the right. The fondly remembered walnut tree stands between Frating Hall and the workshop.

acted as a test laboratory for social and political change in Britain and continues to do so.

The talk was called 'Brightening from the East'. The festival prospectus listed some of the settlements under discussion, one of which was Frating Hall Farm, about which at the time I knew little, and was keen to know more. In the audience were two women, Barbara Thomas and her daughter-in-law Tessa Thomas from Frating Hall Farm itself, Barbara having lived there for more than fifty years with her husband, Martyn Thomas. After the talk they invited my wife Larraine and I to tea. A few weeks later we again found our way there, for the second time in fact. We had visited the farm once before, having been seeing friends in the area, and then only seen it from the outside on a winter's evening in torrential rain. The impression then was of a darkly canopied woodland hideaway, that even if found once might never be found again. This time we went straight there and were made very welcome. That afternoon a number of fascinating documents – recording the history of the farm when it had been managed as a Christian pacifist community between 1943 and 1956, as well as some evocative photographs of the wartime farm during harvesting – were handed round, identified and explained. We were captivated.

'Brightening from the East' reflected my long-standing interest in the symbiotic relationship between London's East End and Essex: in short, the push–pull tension between urban overcrowding and unrest, and rural isolation and sanctuary. This dynamic relationship has always been a crucial factor in the story of how and why Essex became home to so many experiments in living, from the 1880s to this day. There was an additional element which intrigued me, and that was the close relationship between religious and political ideals which seemed to characterise the more successful communal initiatives. It wasn't the Brechtian plea of bread first, morality later, but bread and morality at the same time, preferably on the same plate.

Set on a mixed arable farm in the heart of rural Essex, the story of the Frating Hall community brings together many currents in twentieth-century English social history, eliding political idealism with religious dissent. What follows is a *parti pris* account of one heartening episode in the history of alternative ways of living both within and out of mainstream society (not 'either/or', nor even 'in but not of'), and of relations with others – as friends, family, loved ones and fellow-idealists. Sympathetic to, but also sceptical of Nietzsche's dictum that in history 'there are no facts, only interpretations', in the narrative which follows there are facts for sure, but, based as it is largely on personal recollections, even more interpretations. It is, finally, a story of a belief in the redemptive qualities of work on the land and self-sufficiency in livelihood, in which work is a vocation, imbued with a social as well as an economic purpose.

Unlike histories of other 'experiments in living', to use John Stuart Mill's expressive phrase, this is not a saga of utopian hopes dashed, or paradise lost, but the story of an attempt to live differently in very harsh and socially destructive times. It is the nature of such experiments, as Mill himself understood, that they can't be said to have failed, because their sole raison d'être is to see what works and what doesn't. This is how we learn – in what is a reflexive exercise in communal life and mutual support – to see how people might inhabit spaces and places more convivially together. As one of the children of Frating, Katherine Weaver, remarked in one of our conversations: 'so much of these endeavours are simply unfinished business'.

Farm work allowed the Christian pacifists who established the community at Frating as non-combatants, to remain within the law. Their beliefs already recognised work on the land as a form of political engagement that, unlike so many other utopian prescriptions for changing the world, did not sacrifice the present for the future. Tending the land, growing food and caring for livestock demanded living in the here and now – and sharing that life with others. It was a community which provided a home and a mission in life for members and visitors whose religious and political beliefs had rendered them outsiders in the wider world, a world that was literally at war in every corner of the globe.

The telling of this story is based on understanding the farm as an ideal type, as a way of representing and understanding the 'condition of England question'. In children's picture books the idealised farm has been used to represent human beings and the natural world – especially the animal world – in harmony. With the rise of the novel and other representations of rural life, the family farm continued to provide writers and commentators with a metaphor for the human condition and the nature of the familial estate. Whether as a setting of tragic discomfort, as in the novels of Thomas Hardy, as a place of stoic endurance in Bruce Chatwin's *On the Black Hill*, or as a comic arcadia as depicted in Stella Gibbons' mordant *Cold Comfort Farm*, farm life is life at its most elemental. There is a significant colonial history of farming novels too, mostly written by women as a device to explore the tensions between land, racial exploitation and a yearning for personal freedom: Olive Schreiner's *The Story of an African Farm*, Doris Lessing's *The Grass is Singing*, and more recently Alexandra Fuller's hair-raising *Don't Let's Go to The Dogs Tonight*. Unsurprisingly there are many other variations on the trope, most notably George Orwell's use of it to symbolise a nightmarish dystopia in his bleak satire *Animal Farm*. Coincidentally, Orwell himself flits in and out of these pages in real life.

In recent times the dystopian tide has retreated, giving way to a realisation that smallholding or medium-scale farming can be reimagined and reconstituted once again as a site of ecological and social renewal. Such is the case with Isabella Tree's recent success *Wilding: The Return of Nature to a British Farm*, as well as in James Rebanks' *The Shepherd's Life* and John Lewis-Stempel's *The Running Hare*. Around Britain today there are many experiments in organic and community-based agriculture – and the number is growing all the time. Lessons may be learned, and some are tentatively explored in the conclusion to this book.

I had only just started tracing and interviewing some of those who had grown up at Frating Hall when serious illness intervened at home, followed by the Covid-19 lockdown, keeping Larraine and myself housebound for much of the year. During that time, as I transcribed tapes, photographed documents and ranged the boundless plains of the internet for leads and connections, I realised I too was escaping to Frating: to the triangle of narrow, unmarked lanes, the ancient church and the tree-canopied entrance to the farm estate, ever-present in my mind's eye, comfortingly so. It had become my own 'lost domain', like the forest mansion in the novel *Le Grand Meaulnes*.

In that haunting story, set before the First World War in rural France, which every young person in France is required to read, a young runaway from school stumbles upon a mysterious house set in deep woodland. There he finds a party in full swing, alive with tumblers, magicians, illuminations, music and dancing. The bewitched young outsider stays the night, enchanted by a young woman, promising to return. Alas he is never able to find the mansion again, though he later meets the woman by accident, and marries her. However, the enchantment soon disappears. For me the enchantment of Frating Hall has not gone away. I fell in love with the story and the people who tried to make this ambitious project work against the odds. Others may, too.

Leavening the hard toil of farm work and often needing to survive on a subsistence economy, as well as having to endure widespread disapproval for their pacifist beliefs, Frating also had its own pageants and theatrical enchantments. In addition to the religious rituals and ceremonies, the harvest suppers, the weddings and christenings, the choral concerts and music-making, there were full dress productions of Shakespeare, Synge, T.S. Eliot and other playwrights. Those who farmed by day became actors by night, in motley and greasepaint, entrancing an audience sitting on haystacks in the great barn, lit by Tilley lamps and candles, and where owls hooted and nightingales trilled outside in the woods and fields. These moments, I learnt from those who had grown up there as children, had stayed with them for the rest of their lives.

Folk dancing in the barn at Frating Hall.

Those children and their stories form the substance of this book, and I have attempted to acknowledge all those who helped at the end. However, nothing would have happened without the initial enthusiasm of the original group of people I contacted or who contacted me, namely the late Enid Howard, Barbara Thomas, Martyn Thomas, Phoebe Lambert, Janice Smith (née Watson), Katherine Weaver (née Howard), Patrick Smith, Adam Smith, Peter Watson, John Barrett, Mary Duncan, Kristin Bloom, Rebecca Williams and Paul Burrow. Without their enthusiasm, and the constant encouragement and support of Larraine, this project would not have got off the ground. I am deeply indebted to them all.

Attached is an appendix called 'Prophets of the new world.' This was the title of a Workers' Educational Association (WEA) course once proposed by Frating member Trevor Howard, outlining some of the thinkers and writers whose work informed his religious and political beliefs, and those of his Frating companions. It is a gazetteer of individuals whose writings in the first half of the twentieth century created a constellation of ideas that illuminated the road to a different way of life, that was, in the words of one of the key members of the community, former Durham blast-furnaceman Joe Watson, a 'journey to our heart's desire', in which religious thought productively intersected with radical political action.

In exploring the personal and historical context which led to Frating Hall Farm becoming a pacifist community for a decade, I have been astonished how certain names recur over and again as guiding lights in the memories, letters and writings of those who made a home there. It is clear that those who went there believed unapologetically in the life of the mind and the primacy of the individual conscience – in addition to all the hard work involved in managing a farm and caring for each other. In this world, education was a lifelong endeavour, engaging urgently with the important artistic, philosophical and religious questions of the day. And there were always bicycles at hand: the steadfast engine of social change and happiness then and now.

Many of the names of these once influential thinkers have disappeared into the footnotes of history, but here they are again: Leo Tolstoy, Nikolai Berdyaev, Vera Brittain, Martin Buber, Samuel Koteliansky, D.H. Lawrence, Frank Lea, John Macmurray, Katherine Mansfield, Iris Murdoch, Reinhold Niebuhr, Max Plowman, Karl Polyani, Herbert Read, Richard Rees, Dick Sheppard and Simone Weil, as well, of course, as the mercurial John Middleton Murry. Long before the internet there was an extraordinary geographical and international cultural element to these connections – between the steelworks and mines of north-east England, bohemian London, rural Anglicanism, Russian anarchism, French existentialism and Jewish phenomenology. To paraphrase the artist Jeremy Deller, I am glad that I have lived in a world where these things happened.

1. Politics, letters and the dream of community: John Middleton Murry's *The Adelphi* magazine

> The quest that was to carry Lawrence around the globe was to be the driving-force of Murry's career. Hence, among other things, their recurrent, calamitous attempts, in face of the War, to constitute a community of friends.
>
> FRANK LEA, from *The Life of John Middleton Murry*

The New Life

In one of his letters, D.H. Lawrence, the pre-eminent novelist of Edwardian England, recalled his walks from his home village of Eastwood in Nottinghamshire to Haggs Farm close by, where his first love Jessie Chambers lived, as the happiest time of his life. 'Whatever I forget, I shall never forget the Haggs – I loved it so. I loved to come to you all, it really was a new life began in me there,' he later wrote to Chambers. The memory of a small self-sufficient settlement of family, friends and lovers stayed with him until his death. In 1915 together with the literary critic and socialist John Middleton Murry, by then a close friend, and with Mark Gertler and the Russian Jewish émigré Samuel Koteliansky, Lawrence discussed setting up a utopian community away from the city which was to be called Rananim. In his memoir *Between Two Worlds*, Murry remembered this magical time of 'day-dreaming with Lawrence of the island Rananim, to which we were all to escape from our various miseries'.

In 1915, soon after the outbreak of the First World War, Lawrence and Murry and their partners, Frieda Lawrence and Katherine Mansfield, moved to Zennor in Cornwall and established a communal household there. The experiment was short-lived. Two people as volatile in temperament as Lawrence and his wife were not made for a life of quiet domestic harmony. In a letter written in May 1916 to their mutual friend Koteliansky, Mansfield wrote: 'You may laugh as much as you like at this letter, darling, all about the COMMUNITY. It is rather funny. Frieda and I do not speak to each other at present. Lawrence is about one million miles away, although he lives next door.'

Despite the bad start, Lawrence and Murry remained committed to the dream of living in harmony with nature, far from metropolitan society. This idea – along with related 'back-to-the-land' and 'New Life' impulses – was to be explored in the literary and cultural journal *The Adelphi*, which Murry established in 1923, quickly gaining an enthusiastic readership and following, and is where this story begins. Frieda and Katherine remained close, Frieda giving Mansfield her old wedding ring, which the young writer wore until her death from tuberculosis at the age of thirty-four in 1923, the year *The Adelphi* first saw the light of day. Lawrence never gave up on the dream of getting away from it all, writing to Lady Asquith in 1917 only a year after the Zennor debacle that he still hoped to live 'away from the world, in a little community, a monastery, a school – a little Hesperides of the soul and body'.

The Adelphi was just one of John Middleton Murry's many literary endeavours, each bringing an eclectic constellation of readers and writers into each other's lives. Husband of Mansfield, soulmate of Lawrence (who based Gerald Crich in *Women in Love* on him, according to Frieda), and author of more than sixty books, Murry was not universally admired. Virginia Woolf described him as 'the one vile man I have ever known'. Others who started out as acolytes or fellow enthusiasts also grew disillusioned, as he ricocheted from one new project (and love affair) to another, on what writer H.M. Tomlinson once termed 'the Murry-go-round'. In her brilliant short story 'At the Bay', Katherine Mansfield writes of a household in which, though the woman loves her husband, disaster is often only round the corner: 'There were glimpses, moments, breathing spaces of calm, but all the rest of the time it was like living in a house that couldn't be cured of the habit of catching on fire, on a ship that got wrecked every day.' Those who knew Murry would know exactly what she meant, and where this prescient intuition had come from.

Since then Murry's reputation has waned, but in the first decades of the twentieth century he was regarded as a towering figure in English letters, his reputation gilded by marriage to Mansfield, already a stellar presence on the international literary scene. Although his biographer Frank Lea described him as 'perfectly ill-at-ease in every walk of society', it is nevertheless worth recording that Marcel Proust thought highly of Murry's critical writing and inscribed a volume of *À la recherche du temps perdu* to him, that Lawrence on his deathbed 'had held John's last letter to him in his hand when he was dying', according to Frieda, and that Murry and T.S. Eliot corresponded and kept in touch in later life. It is unlikely that there will ever be a settled position on Murry's talents or character, other than that he was a man of prodigious energy and strong opinions who left a string of unhappy relationships in his wake.

In *Beloved Quixote*, Katherine Murry's memoir of her father, the daughter unpicked the difficult but intense relationship which Murry had with Lawrence, as well as that with his own wife, Katherine Mansfield. In comparison with these two extraordinarily volatile and impassioned personalities, John Middleton Murry seems in retrospect to have remained resolutely earthbound. If they were foxes, to appropriate Isaiah Berlin's dichotomy, he was a hedgehog. Murry's daughter wrote that the tragedy of her father's life lay in 'D.H. Lawrence's unrequited passion for my father, and in my father's idealisation of his first wife Katherine Mansfield.' This was a triangle doomed to failure. The suggestion of Murry's sense of his own inadequacy with respect to Mansfield was confirmed by Murry himself, who confessed that, 'I knew I was her (Mansfield's) inferior in many ways, but I could have accepted them all save one. She had an immediate contact with life which was completely denied to me.'

Despite his many faults, Murry remains central to this story, principally through his advocacy of farming and land settlement as 'community' in action, in the spirit of those early dreams he shared with Lawrence. These aspirations came to fruition at Langham in Essex, where he was instrumental in setting up The Adelphi Centre in 1934. This led in time to a more successful breakaway experiment, in the village of Frating close by, where a small group of Langham dissenters set out to purchase Frating Hall Farm in the autumn of 1942, finally taking full possession in March 1943. This happened largely in reaction to Murry's idiosyncratic and occasionally autocratic behaviour at The Adelphi Centre, and it is the story of the Frating Hall Farm Society which forms the principal subject of this book.

I had first heard of Frating Hall from Enid Howard, then eighty-nine years old, at a lunch organised by conservation architect Shawn Kholucy in January 2012 at his home near Diss. Peter Wells, another Frating member, was also there with his second wife, Jill, together with the architectural historian Gillian Darley. The main topic of conversation was intended to be Enid's and Peter's memories of The Adelphi

Centre, but the conversation soon turned to the breakaway group that went to Frating. It quickly became clear that the story of The Adelphi Centre at Langham had opened a door to a new story entirely, even more fascinating, and that was the story of the Frating Hall Farm. At the time, for a variety of reasons, I was compelled to let the story lapse, until meeting Barbara Thomas and her daughter-in-law Tessa in 2019. Suddenly it became possible to pick up the threads again, with renewed enthusiasm.

A worship of the life force was an expression of the vitalism of the age, and Lawrence was one of its most fervent exponents, and this sentiment is shared by many associated with *The Adelphi* journal, The Adelphi Centre at Langham and eventually at Frating Hall Farm. In his first novel *The White Peacock*, published in 1911 – by chance, the first Lawrence novel I ever read and perhaps for that reason still my favourite – after a discussion of the new French painters and the new music, the narrator's sister Lettie proposes a toast to her companions: '"*To the Vita Nuova!*" said Lettie, and we drank, smiling.'

To be for or against 'life' was the single most important issue that any intellectual or radical thinker could engage with at this time. What is most significant about this ideal is that it was not a call for the revolutionary transformation of the social order, nor a millenarian desire for a perfect world to be revealed by some divine intervention soon. It was a new life that many wanted, more than a new world. The 'New Life' was an aspiration for individuals to learn to live differently in the here and now, not through the wholesale upending of society, but, in Lawrence's words, by building 'new little habitats', with 'new little hopes'.

The editorial in the first edition of *The Adelphi* asserted 'that life is important and that more life should be man's chief endeavour'. 'Life is marvellous. I want to be deeply rooted in it – to live – to expand – to breathe in it – to rejoice – to share it,' wrote Katherine Mansfield in one of her letters. Not only was there 'life' in its existential essence – a more agnostic version of Sir Thomas Browne's axiom that 'Life is a pure flame and we live with an invisible sun within us' – but there was the 'New Life', a syncretic programme of new ways of living that would revolutionise and harmonise the world, but only once the shackles of bourgeois conformity had been cast aside. Such ideas had been circulating in intellectual circles since the 1870s. They are agonised over in the plays of Ibsen and Chekhov, and celebrated by the Freudians and the Theosophists. Thoughts of the New Life or New Age to come gave comfort to the early feminists and pioneers of homosexual equality, to child pedagogy, to the advocates of *lebensreform* (a potent mixture of vegetarianism, naturism, rational dress and free sexual relations), to the anti-vivisectionists, as well as to expressionism in the arts and living in harmony with nature. But most potently, the New Life could only be fully achieved in a new kind of community – of people and of place.

Back to the land: Tolstoy in Essex

To this largely secular history must be added the extraordinary influence of the Russian writer Leo Tolstoy across the world at this time. In addition to his reputation as a novelist – *War and Peace* was published in 1869, *Anna Karenina* in 1878 – the writer was admired for the tenacity of his Christian pacifism and anti-militarism, as well as support for the rural peasantry and their way of life, free of the yoke of serfdom against which he had ardently campaigned. His writings on these and other matters were circulated internationally, which, allied to his ascetic lifestyle, caused some to regard him almost as a 'second Christ'.

In 1884 Tolstoy had published a long essay called 'What I Believe', initially prompted by his profound opposition to Tsarist conscription, in which he also promulgated the idea of non-violent resistance to all forms of oppression, whether by the state or any other form of arbitrary authority or power. 'Without Tolstoy there would have been no Gandhi, no Archbishop Tutu, no Nelson Mandela,' suggested A.N. Wilson in his biography of the writer. One could also add: no Martin Luther King, no American civil rights movement, no Committee of 100, no Greenham Common Women's Camp, or many of the other exercises in non-violent civil disobedience which have today become a central part of the repertoire of peaceful protest across the world, even if Tolstoy's original prescriptions were enlarged to suit new circumstances. This suggestion is confirmed by one of the Frating members, Phoebe Lambert, who went on in later life to study the impact of pacifist beliefs on her parents and their generation, concluding that 'The pacifist movement has, through its commitment to non-violence and to the importance of reflection and dialogue, had a lasting influence on the civil-rights and anti-apartheid movements across the world.' This was no small achievement.

More than this though was Tolstoy's insistence that what one believed was no indication of moral worth compared to the simple question of how one lived. In this regard the central element of the Christian faith to Tolstoy and his followers was the simplicity of the life that Jesus had lived and the morality he practised in his life and teachings. Hence the injunction to turn the other cheek when threatened with violence, hence the injunction to love one's enemy, allied to the disdain for wealth and material things in comparison with love for one's fellow beings. Tolstoy's anarchism derived directly from these principles, rejecting the actions of the political insurrectionists as much as the aspirations of the liberals who sought to gain power by democratic means in order to change society from above. 'Only one thing remains,' he wrote in his diary on 7 February 1895, 'to fight the Government with weapons of thought, word and way of life, not making any concessions to it, not joining its ranks, not increasing its powers oneself.' The poet Rilke put it just as simply, but rather more famously in his poem 'Archaic Torso of Apollo', with its concluding dictum, 'You must change your life'.

Tolstoy was the 'New Life' incarnate. His religious and political writings attracted the admiration of the Quakers, in Britain and North America – and Quakers play an important part in this story – as did his support for the ideas of the then increasingly influential economist Henry George, whose advocacy of the communal ownership of land as a precondition for more equal, self-governing communities, was gaining interest and support across the world, as it is once again today. Largely overlooked until very recently, it is arguable that it was Henry George rather than Karl Marx who had the greater impact on popular ideas of socialism at the end of the nineteenth century. It was George's theories on land value and land taxation that fuelled the 'back-to-the-land' sentiments increasingly adopted by radicals such as William Morris, Robert Blatchford and George Lansbury in Britain, as well as amongst the religious social reformers of the settlement movement.

Given that this story concerns one such back-to-the-land experiment, that at Frating, it is appropriate that Tolstoy's writings on the land question first entered Britain via a farm cottage close by, at Purleigh, a hamlet on Essex's Dengie Peninsula. Thus, Tolstoy's ideas did not have far to travel, even if the journey took some time. It was at Purleigh that a small utopian community had been established by the Brotherhood Church in 1896, under the benign leadership of John Coleman Kenworthy, a Tolstoyan follower and fellow anarchist. Having corresponded with the great novelist, Kenworthy went to Russia in 1895 to meet the man himself and sign an arrangement to publish English translations of some of Tolstoy's shorter books and essays.

In the same year that the Purleigh colony was established, Tolstoy's celebrated translators Aylmer and Louise Maude had set up house at Wickham's Farm nearby. They too were keen supporters of Kenworthy's utopian experiment. Soon Tolstoy's right-hand man Vladimir Chertkov arrived too, establishing home for a while in order to strengthen the connection between Tolstoy and his English supporters. It was Chertkov who kept Tolstoy up to date with events in England, sharing his interest in the work of the Salvation Army, who in 1891 set up the Hadleigh Farm Colony in Essex as a rehabilitation scheme for the poor of east London. While in Essex, Chertkov began organising aid for the beleaguered Russian Christian sect the Doukhobors, then being harshly persecuted by the Tsar for their pacifist beliefs. Soon after, a small group of the traditionally dressed Doukhobors arrived in England and came to stay at Purleigh, causing considerable difficulties for the colonists with their rural neighbours, as the strangely robed Russians were quickly rumoured to be anarchists in disguise, arriving 'with snow on their boots', as the saying goes.

Tolstoy's influence in Britain was compounded not only by Chertkov's residence in Essex. After leaving Purleigh, Chertkov went to Bournemouth and there established a full-blown Tolstoyan colony at Tuckton House, Iford, where for a number of years all of Tolstoy's original manuscripts were gathered and stored, having been smuggled out of Russia. It was this collection of original manuscripts that formed the basis for the definitive ninety-volume edition of Tolstoy's works, later published in Russia. They had been kept in a fireproof strongroom, with eighteen-inch-thick concrete walls lined with firebricks, and a steel entry door. When Tuckton House was levelled in 1965 for redevelopment, it took two workmen a full week to gain entry to the strongroom before it could be demolished. Here Chertkov and his fellow anarchists kept Tolstoy's writing safe from Tsarism and Bolshevism.

So it was from Bournemouth – through the Free Age Press they established in that genteel seaside town – that Tolstoy's followers printed tens of thousands of copies of the great man's essays and teachings to be circulated throughout Britain and beyond, many priced at a penny a copy. Wilson notes that 'Though his name was famous abroad, *War and Peace* and *Anna Karenina* were barely known in the West. It was through his religious tracts that, for thousands of English readers, Tolstoy burst upon the world.' Some of those tracts were to have a great impact on the Langham settlers and the Frating pacifists in particular.

There are other mythologies in the long but episodic story of the back-to-the-land movement in Essex. One is that following the agricultural depression of the 1870s the county's agriculture was saved by the 'Redeeming Scots', an influx of farmers from Scotland who came down by train with their cattle from Ayrshire, and transformed cereal-based farming into a dairy culture. By supplying the London capital with all the milk needed for its fast-growing population, the story is that they turned a failing industry into a commercial success. The Scots were, one historian has said, 'as devoted to pasture as Essex men were to cereals', and 'the chief cause of Essex becoming a dairy county'. The result was that by the mid-twentieth century Scottish newcomers farmed somewhere approaching half of Essex and were prominent in the local agricultural community. For some reason the parishes of Frating, Lawford, Bradfield and Little Bromley –

which together constitute the Tendring Hundred – remained relatively impervious to Scottish farming ownership, despite being once described as 'amongst the finest farming land in England with ready access to rail transport'. The tradition of mixed stock and arable farming therefore continued on the Tendring peninsula, and it was this tradition that the Langham group found when they arrived at Frating Hall Farm, and proceeded to cultivate.

Other developments in land settlement at this time originated with rather different social aims. These were principally to provide work for unemployed Londoners and their families away from the East End slums, usually managed in a paternalist way by religious or public bodies as 'land colonies'. The Salvation Army was already one of the most successful, establishing in 1890 a 'Land and Industrial Colony', at Hadleigh, overlooking the Thames close to the estuary, still operating today, more than a hundred and thirty years later. This was the one Tolstoy's agent Chertkov found especially interesting.

One influential figure of this first wave was Thomas Smith, who by the end of his life had garnered an international reputation for his outstanding contribution to horticulture. Under the spell of Robert Blatchford's 1894 manifesto 'Merrie England', Smith settled with his family in Mayland, Essex on the River Blackwater in 1895 determined to create a new arcadia. The venture attracted the attention of Fabian Society enthusiasts such as George Lansbury, Joseph Rowntree and American-born soap manufacturer and philanthropist, Joseph Fels. It was Fels who, after meeting and being impressed by Smith, underwrote the expansion of the Mayland colony, subsequently buying 600 acres of farmland, which he divided up into twenty-one separate smallholdings. Within a few years the Mayland experiment was growing its own food, producing its own meat and dairy products, and providing homes and a school, along with other social amenities, for the colonists, most of whom were unemployed Londoners and their families. It also exported produce to London by way of a short rail link to a river jetty on the Blackwater, where boats could moor at high tide and from there set sail around the coast.

In 1909 Smith's book *French Gardening* was published by Fels under the imprint of the Utopia Press, with an introduction by Kropotkin. It became one of the most influential works on market gardening ever written. He followed it in 1913 with *The Profitable Culture of Vegetables*. These works earned him an international reputation, with an RHS Gold Medal being later awarded 'in recognition of the work you have done for horticulture and in particular as the author of that magnificent book *The Profitable Culture of Vegetables*'. Smith died in 1955, and is buried in Mayland church, a major figure in the history of English agriculture and market gardening.

The Society of Friends – commonly known today as the Quakers – also began to take an interest in supporting such smallholding schemes in England after the First World War. Known as 'Group Holdings', and aimed at unemployed miners, the first scheme was launched at Potton in Bedfordshire, but soon came to north-east Essex. This led subsequently to the formation of the Land Settlement Association (LSA) in 1932, able to attract government funding. According to Marina O'Connell, a smallholder herself, the LSA:

> bought up farms across the country and divided them into groups of 50–80 holdings of 4–10 acres each. Each holding had a modern home and was equipped with piggeries, chicken sheds, machinery sheds, glasshouses and more. Approximately 1000 holdings were created over 21 sites. They were to be run as 'colonies' (their terminology) and miners were 'settled' on the holdings and given basic training to

> become smallholders. This was viewed as either; the first step to emigration to further flung colonies like New Zealand, or the first step on to the farming ladder. The Estates had central stores and pack-houses and were run as 'compulsory cooperatives'. The tenant had to sell the produce they grew through the pack-house and these crops were grown according to a centralised cropping programme for ease of marketing. In this way the LSA hoped to overcome the inefficiencies of the small-sized plot.

One drawback to the scheme was that most of the sites selected for conversion to smallholdings were in the south of England, yet were aimed at recruiting unemployed miners from the North East. In a short time Ardleigh became a regional stronghold for market gardening. Remnants of it are still evident today in a scattering of glasshouses, vegetable and flower beds, orchards and outbuildings, a few of which remain in commercial use.

For a while, another key figure in this story, Hugh Barrett, worked for the LSA in Essex. He came to realise that some of the miners and other unemployed workers from the north of England were finding it difficult to settle in a working environment that was by tradition paternalistic, whether working for private farm-owners or for a government scheme. As he wrote in his late-in-life memoir *A Good Living*:

> Considering the kind of people responsible for the LSA organisation, it is not surprising that from the outset they failed to recognise that the North Country man, especially the miner, was entirely different from the rural East Anglian worker. Miners are traditionally both independent and inter-dependent: to survive they had to be. They had a sense of personal and corporative worth. They would not be patronised by anyone.

O'Connell goes on to describe the social conditions smallholders had to abide by, noting that 'the holdings were set up as market gardens growing salads, vegetables and fruit with a small amount of livestock in the form of pigs and poultry. The allotments were equipped with tools, outbuildings, stock and glasshouses and, importantly, a home.' They were also strictly supervised, with the newly equipped market gardeners monitored for timekeeping by an Estate Manager, and wages dispensed in instalments. From her interviews with a number of people who grew up on these smallholdings, O'Connell concluded that the women and children were the happiest in these new surroundings, but the men missed the comradeship of the workplace and the pub, and, for some, the chapel.

Surprisingly, it was a Conservative government which after regaining power from Labour in 1951 revived the Land Settlement Association, keen to encourage the unemployed to get back to the land. The area around Lawford and Ardleigh in Essex once again became a major focus for the creation of new smallholdings, orchards and market gardens. At their high point, the LSA gardens 'provided about 78% of salad in the UK wholesale market,' according to O'Connell. Eventually cheap imports of food started to arrive in the UK, and the growing power of the supermarkets began a race to the bottom in terms of price and quality, and so the LSA declined, finally coming to an end in the 1980s.

> When the holdings were in full flow in the 60s and 70s people use the words idyllic, utopia, paradise over and over. Hard work yes, but also a time of friendships, community and making a good living. People who were children at that time told stories of how they 'free ranged' across the holdings with other children, how their parents were there on site, but very busy. The generation that were the growers in

> the 1960s and 1970s told me stories of collaboration on the holdings. How they shared knowledge and information freely as they were not competing with each other. One retired grower told me very proudly about how they experimented with their crops from very high skill base and not from an intellectual or college base.

It was a significant episode in modern agricultural history, and it is within this history of land settlement schemes that the socialists and pacifists associated with John Middleton Murry added their own distinctive contribution as war loomed at the end of the 1930s, that 'low, dishonest decade'.

From left to right: the young Shirley Williams (née Catlin), Derek Crosfield, Raymond Smith and Helen Johnson on a potato planter, Frating Hall Farm, 1948.

2. Swords into ploughshares

> War is a crime against humanity. I renounce war, and am therefore determined not to support any kind of war. I am also determined to work for the removal of all causes of war.
>
> THE PEACE PLEDGE, 1936

Success for The Adelphi

As a journal *The Adelphi* proved a great success. It attracted readers from across the country and from all walks of life, and Lawrence's writings featured prominently from the beginning, not surprisingly since Murry later admitted that he had started the magazine 'primarily so he could publish Lawrence's work in it'. Murry also used the magazine to promote the work of his wife Katherine Mansfield, who had recently died tragically young. Yet apart from its literary focus, the journal also put matters of social reform and even spiritual and religious questions to the fore, including an early preoccupation with what is now termed communitarianism and 'the art of right living'. In an advertisement for the first edition of *The Adelphi*, Vol. 1, No. 1, June 1923, the first three feature essays are by Middleton Murry ('The Cause of it All'), Katherine Mansfield ('The Samuel Josephs'), and D.H. Lawrence ('Trees and Babies and Papas and Mamas'), respectively.

Among *The Adelphi*'s early and most enthusiastic readers was a Newcastle blast-furnaceman Joe Watson, who along with other fellow-subscribers amongst the Northumbrian miners and steelworkers he mixed with, became a convinced follower of the journal's new aesthetic and social agenda, with its strong Christian socialist leanings. Many years later, in 1962, four years before dying in a car crash on 12 September 1966, Watson wrote a short essay for *Ambit* poetry magazine on what *The Adelphi* magazine had meant to him: 'From the first number *The Adelphi* was meant to be more than just another magazine. It was to be a commentary on life: an introduction to what life could be: the expression of intense personal relationship.'

In another short essay, on this occasion written after Murry's death, Watson recalled his first encounter with Murry's writings and ideas. 'I first heard of Middleton Murry in 1923. A gang of us were erecting a headgear and screening plant for a new pit, working long hours, seven days a week, and during the meal times politics, religion and books were discussed, and the name of Murry and his new *Adelphi* magazine was introduced. We were split on the Lawrence–Murry controversy,' Watson wrote, 'although all of us read Murry fervently in spite of it.' The controversy Watson is referring to here arose when *The Adelphi* published extracts from Lawrence's *Fantasia of the Unconscious*, which was taken by a number of readers to be blasphemous, written by an author who some claimed had 'spat in the face of Jesus'.

'A number of working men were gathered around Murry by this time,' Watson continued. 'I was a blast-furnaceman, and cotton workers, plasterers, railwaymen and others were there, also a few hangers on.' He later remembered walking along the street of a small industrial town with another *Adelphi* reader, who, from time to time, stopped those he knew to announce: 'A new asceticism is upon us.' The enthusiast then hauled the magazine out of his pocket and added, 'It has it here.' There was clearly something radical and life-affirming in the air.

Joe Watson was one of those who did not fall by the wayside or wholly recant on his devotion to Murry as others were to do at this time – and here the religious vocabulary is apt – though the two did eventually fall out over financial matters. Like other working-class *Adelphi* readers in his circle, Watson was not only a socialist but a devout Christian. A self-educated man who had left school at the age of twelve, he ran a weekly book group at the steelworks in Consett where he and his fellow workers read and discussed Keats and Shakespeare, Lawrence and Marx, galvanised by *The Adelphi* magazine and its essays, short stories and poems. Yet for Watson it was the combination of religion and politics that captured him: 'If God and politics mattered, then politics mattered. Hence the quotation from Blake which eventually appeared on the front of *The Adelphi*: "Religion is politics and politics is brotherhood."' Watson also noted that the Greek word *adelphi* means brothers, or siblings – those from the same womb.

If Watson was a commanding personality, in Murry he encountered a kindred spirit. Finally meeting Murry in person in 1936 at an *Adelphi* summer school, Watson later wrote of himself that he 'had been a disciple of his for fourteen years'. In a similar vein, a railwayman who once stopped Watson in the street said to him, 'I believe you know Middleton Murry. He is my arch-priest.' Recalling that first meeting, Watson later remembered Murry as:

> A dark, slightly built man, thin on top, with a lined face which was to become more lined as the years went by. He looked very frail to my eye, deceptively so, for he had a workmanlike approach to a practical job which would have got him work anywhere. When digging a garden he had a clean style, and the finished plot was of a professional standard. He was no cack-handed fumbler. The spade went into the ground the full depth of the blade, with a great economy of effort, the hallmark of good digging.

Few people would judge a character principally on the way they handled a spade, but, ever the practical man of action, Watson did. He found not only an intellectual hero but a fellow workman, a man who enjoyed the company of working-class people, while holding fast to his beliefs in the leavening effects of education and collective self-determination.

Other workers in the North East found a political and spiritual home in *The Adelphi* too, including Durham miner Sid Chaplin, and Jack Common, both of whom went on to write critically acclaimed novels, short stories and essays. Chaplin was to become feted as a significant literary original who had emerged self-fashioned from difficult beginnings. His first collection of short stories, *The Leaping Lad*, was published in 1946, and he went on to write seven novels, all well-received, including *The Thin Seam* in 1949 and *The Day of the Sardine* in 1961, giving him a national literary reputation. All three men, Chaplin, Common and Watson, had been reared in a culture in which radical politics, internationalism, literary aspirations and the cause of working-class adult education were taken seriously. Chaplin and Watson remained close friends for nearly forty years until Watson's death in 1966, as did their respective families, and then afterwards. Sid Chaplin's son, contemporary playwright Michael Chaplin, still speaks warmly of his 'Uncle' Joe Watson, remembering the larger-than-life figure his father so admired.

Jack Common, son of a Tyneside railwayman, sometime clerk, a socialist, another early *Adelphi* reader and would-be poet, was subsequently taken up by Murry as an editorial assistant on the magazine. Befriended by George Orwell, now a regular *Adelphi* contributor, Common and Orwell soon became close too. The latter writer, an Old Etonian who had taken up the banner of democratic socialism and always on the lookout for the authentic proletarian writer, quickly realised that Common was the real thing. Common published two fine novels, *Kiddar's Luck* and *The Ampersand,* as well as editing two collections of essays, *The Freedom of the Streets* (which V.S. Pritchett thought was one of the best books he had ever read) *Seven Shifts*, an anthology of essays by different people about the work they did. Common enjoys an unusual but enduring memorial: the bust of Karl Marx in Highgate Cemetery was partly modelled on the stocky Tynesider's features by sculptor Laurence Bradshaw.

Pacifism, the new agrarianism and some strange bedfellows

Exhausted by his efforts in running the magazine, together with the many other projects he was to become involved with, Murry eventually decided to find a new owner for *The Adelphi* after the Second World War. The person who bought it was the writer and occasional contributor, Henry Williamson, whose first contribution for *The Adelphi* had been published in September 1924, an essay called 'The Doom of the Peregrine Falcon'. Yet a decade later Williamson's admiration for Hitler and close friendship and political association with Oswald Mosley – sympathies and affiliations Williamson never recanted – was causing great concern in liberal and left-wing circles, but on rural matters the 1930s produced some strange bedfellows. In this period countryside interests and causes attracted both right-wing and left-wing adherents and commentators.

A somewhat unexpected example can be found in an editorial in the journal *Criterion*, published in 1938, in which the poet T.S. Eliot, by self-definition, a 'classicist in literature, royalist in politics, and anglo-catholic in religion', proposed that:

> To have the right frame of mind it is not enough that we should read Wordsworth, tramp the countryside with a book of British Birds and a cake of chocolate in a ruck-sack, or even own a country estate: it is necessary that the greater part of the population, of all classes (so long as we have classes) should be settled in the country and dependent upon it.

In the words of Alexandra Harris's acute summary of Eliot's stance: 'He had done his research and was absolutely serious. England's most prominent poet was advocating a vast, co-ordinated return to the soil.' A year later – the year that war was declared – Eliot published a collection of essays under the title of 'The Idea of a Christian Society', which idealised the image of the self-sufficient Christian rural retreat. Middleton Murry and Eliot had been in touch with each other for many years, and towards the end of their lives corresponded frequently, even though Murry was by then becoming a marginal and disparaged figure.

This sharing of disputed ideological territory is evident in the list of contributors to *The Adelphi* after the war, whether under Murry's or Williamson's editorship, when articles and essays by anarchists such as Herbert Read and George Woodcock rubbed shoulders with essays by Williamson and Rolf Gardiner, both expressing sympathies for 'blood and soil' atavism. Lawrence of course was of all parties and none, creating allies and enemies across the full range of the political spectrum. This regressive world of rural politics has recently been explored in Melissa Harrison's disturbing novel *All Among the Barley*, which digs deep and painfully into matters of land and loyalty and their political affiliations between the wars.

The curious admixture of political and religious cross-currents is evident in another journal to which Murry, Common and others contributed called – highly problematically to modern ears – *The Aryan Path*. When I first came across advertisements for the magazine in archive copies of the *Times Literary Supplement*, alarm bells rang because of the title. In fact, the journal, published in Bombay, ran from 1930 to 1960, was an Anglo-Indian collaboration established to explore a range of spiritual and social issues which had their origins in Theosophy, but was eclectic in its range of contributors. Apart from Murry and Common, other contributors included Arthur Waley, G.D.H. Cole, Ramananda Chatterjee, C.E.M. Joad and Mark Benney (a former Soho burglar who became a regular columnist for the *New Statesman* and ended up as a Professor of Sociology at the University of Chicago). The search for the new life ranged far and wide.

Swords into ploughshares

The decade of the 1930s was clearly a period of considerable intellectual and political turmoil. Disillusionment with the carnage of the First World War had inspired a growing pacifist movement culminating in the formation of the Peace Pledge Union (PPU) in 1934. There was already one eminent pacifist in Essex, Sir Norman Angell, living on Northey Island close to Maldon. Angell's 1910 book *The Great Illusion* foresaw the First World War and urged the need for European economic cooperation. Internationally admired for his global perspectives on diplomacy and negotiation, Angell was awarded the Nobel Peace Prize in 1933. Pacifism was now finding supporters in all corners of Britain and amongst all classes, whether in revulsion against the horrors of the last 'war to end all wars', or in fear of the next to come.

The poet Max Plowman, another Murry follower, was said to have been responsible for converting Murry to the pacifist cause. Born in 1883, Plowman had fought in the First World

War and been badly wounded. Appalled by the horrors of the war, he refused to return to duties on being discharged from treatment, was tried as a conscientious objector, acquitted and dismissed from the army. In 1930 he joined Murry and Richard Rees, an Old Etonian aristocrat and philosopher and stalwart of the Workers' Educational Association – and who later drove ambulances for the Republicans during the Spanish Civil War – to assist on *The Adelphi* magazine. Both were enthusiastic followers of the charismatic Anglican priest and Dean of Canterbury, Dick Sheppard, who was to play an important part in the lives of many in this story. Plowman had been closely involved in the setting up of the PPU in 1936, where he established the 'Forethought Committee', one of whose principal objectives was advocating farm work and humanitarian aid as an alternative to military conscription.

Many of the men associated with *The Adelphi* journal and who found themselves turning towards the pacifist cause in the 1930s did so from experience, not ideology. They had fought in the First World War and several had been seriously injured, others decorated for bravery. Widespread disillusionment with the appalling death toll of the First World War, allied to economic distress in the UK and the rise of fascism in Germany, Spain and Italy gave an urgency to new ideas in social reform, including 'New Life' elements and pacifist ideas, though this was not to last. There was also a renewed interest in political and religious communitarianism – often encouraged and promulgated by the PPU – with its concern for a return to the land as the source of peace and well-being. This was allied with an interest in spiritualism and even quasi-religious mysticism, particularly amongst the educated middle classes, on which matter Orwell was famously – and disproportionately, many would say – scathing. Orwell's dismissal of 'New Life' concerns came despite the fact that many fellow *Adelphi* contributors were now taking an interest in less materialistic ways of thinking, including former communists such as Iris Murdoch.

Religious and philosophical ideas were becoming more widely discussed as a result of the publication in England of the writings of philosophers such as Nikolai Berdyaev, Jacques Maritain, Martin Buber and Reinhold Niebuhr, and latterly, Simone Weil, whose ideas were beginning to find a receptive audience in *The Adelphi* and elsewhere. Yet what was perhaps most unexpected, though in retrospect completely understandable, was the overlap between pacifism and agrarianism, which was not only promulgated by the PPU. In addition to Plowman's enthusiasm for agricultural communes, Methodist minister and PPU member Henry Carter had started to organise the Christian Pacifist Forestry and Land Units. In his essay on the history of *The Adelphi* magazine, critic Michael H. Whitworth wrote that, 'By the 1940s, the journal was calling for a national renaissance based on an agricultural renaissance, a position derived from Murry's pacifism.' Pacifism and agrarianism were now seen to be part of the same new world view.

Apart from initiatives at Langham and Frating, described in detail shortly, elsewhere in Essex pacifists chose to go back to the land. In a moving collection of short memoirs of their lives as conscientious objectors during the Second World War written by 'Friends of Colchester and Coggeshall Monthly Meeting', two contributors reflect on such experiences. Hugh Clunes recalls that a Chelmsford Quaker and businessman on declaration of war promptly sold his family home and bought a 150-acre farm nearby where 'he would employ as many COs [conscientious objectors] as possible and the group would live together as a community with free board and lodging and a little pocket money'. The farm soon was able to provide work and shelter for eight adults and three children. Bill Skinner, then a Methodist, 'decided to follow my ancestors onto the land and went to a small community farm at Clavering in Essex run by War Resisters International'. Not all COs faced public disapproval all of the time. Hospital worker Albert Pike tells a remarkable story. 'One memory sticks out: the number of men who came up to shake my hand when I registered as a CO at Romford Labour Exchange in 1940. All eyes were on me when I walked forward to answer the clerk's shout of "Where's that CO?" I'm sure he was as surprised as I was at the reception I got from the crowd.'

In 1947 anarchist George Woodcock – friend and later biographer of Orwell, a pacifist who would spend much of the Second World War working on a farm in Suffolk – published a short book, *The Basis of Communal Living*. This described the growth of pacifist sentiments in Britain in the 1930s, and the transformation of these sentiments into the practical business of setting up self-sufficient communities:

> In the years before and during the war, there has been a strong movement to found communities in Britain, arising largely out of the peculiar circumstances of the British pacifist movement at the beginning of the war. The communities which arose during this period were numerous, running into several hundreds. Some lasted only a few months – others are still alive and thriving after seven or eight years. Their sizes range from two or three up to a hundred members; their theoretical approaches were equally varied, ranging from Christian mysticism to materialist anarchism, while they presented a variety of economic structures, and their functions ranged from farming units to living communities in towns, from free schools to travelling theatre groups. The majority, however, were connected in some way with agriculture.

The Reverend Dick Sheppard, already mentioned, played a pivotal role in many other lives apart from that of Plowman and Murry. His public self-questioning dominated theological discussions in the Anglican church for decades. Born in 1880, educated at Cambridge, ordained in 1908 whilst working at Oxford House Settlement in Bethnal Green, Sheppard (full name Hugh Richard Lawrie Sheppard) eventually became Dean of Canterbury. He had been a chaplain in France during the First World War where he suffered the first of a number of personal crises or breakdowns. In 1924 he gave the first of what were to become many religious talks on BBC Radio, the energy and passion of which turned him into a national figure. By now a confirmed pacifist, he was the beating heart of the PPU which quickly gained over 100,000 members, all of whom were required to sign the pledge given at the head of this chapter. In the event, it is estimated that about 60,000 of those called up refused to bear arms as conscientious objectors, a surprisingly higher figure than might have been expected. Some went to prison, some served in the medical corps, and others worked in 'reserved occupations' such as mining or farming.

It was Dick Sheppard again who was responsible for converting the writer and social reformer Vera Brittain to pacifism. Brittain was renowned as the author of *Testament of Youth*, published in 1933, her disillusioned account of the impact of the First World War on the women and families left bereaved or shattered by family breakdown was controversial but touched a national nerve. 'She served three years (as a Voluntary Aid Detachment nurse) in England, Malta and France,' recorded her biographer Muriel Melldown, 'during which time she experienced at first hand the horrors of modern warfare. By the end of the war her fiancé, her brother, and her two closest friends were dead.'

The high public regard she enjoyed following the publication of *Testament of Youth* did not however protect her from the opprobrium she received from the press on proclaiming her conversion to pacifism. The contempt and disgrace which trailed her endless campaigning took a high toll on her morale as yet another devastating war drew closer. She later wrote in a second memoir, *Testament of Experience*: 'To follow Dick meant treading the Way of the Cross in a modern guise. He pointed to a path which might end, not in crucifixion or a den of lions, but at internment, the concentration camp, and the shooting squad.' It would be hard to overestimate the intensity of the moral turmoil that the prospect of another world war caused the liberal wing of the Anglican church or many of the nonconformist denominations, a religious anguish in the face of war relatively muted today.

In 1925 Brittain had married the political scientist George Catlin. They had a son, John in 1927, and a daughter, Shirley in 1930. Her close association with Plowman and the PPU eventually brought her into contact with the Murry and the *Adelphi* group, and it was in this way that she first came to Langham in Essex where Murry and Plowman had established The Adelphi Centre. Though Brittain never resided permanently at Langham, she became interested in the idea of establishing an agricultural community, and the opportunity came when The Adelphi Centre at Langham closed, and she offered financial support to one of its successors, the one to be set up at Frating.

Brittain's association with Sheppard marked her life, and her death. In the crypt of St Martin-in-the-Fields, Trafalgar Square, there is a Dick Sheppard Chapel containing a plaque with the words 'Blessed are the Peacemakers', dedicated to the memory of Vera Brittain. Sheppard himself had died suddenly in 1937 resulting in an outpouring of public consternation and grief, and, in the process, leaving the PPU without its charismatic figurehead. In a letter written by Middleton Murry to Joe Watson on 4 November 1937, Murry recorded: 'I've just returned from the funeral service to Dick Sheppard at St Paul's – a cold house of God if ever there was one, but made warm by the love of thousands of ordinary people.' In the same letter he renews a discussion with Watson over the nature of communal living, both looking back to the Middle Ages for inspiration, though to different traditions, guild and monastic.

The sociologist Dennis Hardy, to whom students of the British utopian tradition owe much, suggests that behind the pacifist enthusiasm for rural self-sufficient communities lay the model of the monastery. 'It is in many ways the ultimate utopian community, a sanctuary in a troubled world, and offers its members a unique balance of intellectual and physical activity.' The religious sentiment behind the growth of the pacifist cause was evident in the commonly expressed wish to establish 'cells of good living'. But when war threatened once again towards the end of the 1930s, a return to the monastery did not seem the best way of coming to the aid of one's fellow men and women. Nonetheless in a letter to his wife Katherine Mansfield shortly before she died, John Middleton Murry had described himself as 'a monk without a monastery'. For those who did not wish to pick up a sword, the only thing to do was to put one's hand to the plough. Instead of a return to the monastery, there was now a return to the farm.

The Oaks, Langham, Essex. From 1934 to 1942 the buildings and land were managed by John Middleton Murry and Max Plowman as The Adelphi Centre, a residential socialist and community land project.

3. 'Low living and high thinking'

So politics it must be. But one needs to be disinfected night and morning.

JOHN MIDDLETON MURRY in a letter to Clare Farr, 21 July 1933

The Adelphi Centre

The Adelphi Centre started out as an experiment in communal self-sufficiency and socialist education in order to promote the cause of *The Adelphi* journal: in other words, to practise what it preached. Having originally tried and failed to find suitable premises in Derbyshire, where Murry had strong links with the Independent Labour Party, he decided upon East Anglia, and on 10 September 1935 Murry came across The Oaks, a large private nineteenth-century mansion with land attached in the hamlet of Langham in Essex, close to Colchester. The cost of the house, with an adjoining cottage and two fields was £2,475, of which Murry invested £1000 of his own as share capital.

Under Plowman and Murry's stewardship it first operated under the name of The Adelphi Centre. The idea of a new kind of radical settlement or college was first mooted by Murry at a summer school for *The Adelphi* magazine, and, according to Murry, the response there was sufficient 'to encourage me to go ahead'. In his sympathetic biography of Murry, philosopher and literary critic Frank Lea cannot but help connect Murry's enthusiasm for establishing this new domestic and educational settlement with the ghastly failure of his own personal circumstances, having not for the first time been required to flee from his own home due to marital discord. It would seem that a number of the first members of this new experiment in education and community were also escaping from similarly difficult personal circumstances. This did not presage a good start.

Murry later summarised the aims of the Centre thus:

> The Adelphi Centre will be a training centre for making socialists – but real socialists not socialist 'politicians'. We believe that the essential element in the making of socialists is almost wholly neglected. This essential element is 'education into community'. This education cannot, in the nature of things, be theoretical merely. It is, we think, self-evident that it can be accomplished only by actual cooperation in ordinary human work. No such socialist centre can be really living until each member, or guest, takes as an obvious duty his full share, according to his capacity, of the actual work of the place; nor can it be truly healthy until it becomes largely self-supporting in the simple necessities of life.

This summary seems to be little more than a boiling down of Marx's dictum, 'From each according to their ability, to each according to their needs,' though Murry intended to make the word flesh. He provided a lively if partisan account of the Centre's ambitions in a full-length memoir and justification of his 'back-to-the-land' philosophy in his book *Community Farm*, published in 1953. This was an *apologia pro vita sua*, a defence of his life's work as ill health becalmed him. Issued four years before he died in 1957, Murry wrote that he had read Marx and admired his analysis of capitalism's faults, but was worried by the 'apocalyptic, eschatological streak in him'. Deeply sceptical of the Soviet Union's experiment in state-controlled collectivism, he saw it as possessing a similar apocalyptic millenarianism. Murry believed in democracy, but was equally sceptical about Labour's strategy of nationalisation, and concluded that only producer cooperatives could provide the democratic way forward. This was notably the case with regard to the stewardship of the land and the production of food. 'I believe service to the land is an unconditional good,' he wrote in *Community Farm*. Murry concluded the same book with the earnest plea that 'Agriculture offers perhaps the best and most natural opportunity for the development of a new sense of responsibility.'

However, the project struggled from the beginning. There was little farming experience amongst the first recruits and the land was poor; Murry came and went, busy with other projects and commitments. In 1937, the farming aspect of the Centre was terminated and the building handed back to the PPU, under whose auspices it was used as a home for more than fifty Basque children arriving in May 1937, refugees from the Spanish Civil War. In an article called 'Under the Oak Tree' written for *Peace News* and published on 12 June 1937, Plowman's wife Dorothy described the setting:

> Five miles out of Colchester on the Ipswich Road a fine old oak in the middle of a grass triangle marks a turning on the left leading to the hamlet of Langham. This local landmark is known as the Langham Oak. Following the turning (and bearing first right then left) for about half a mile, the traveller comes on a solidly built, comfortable-looking house of grey stone standing in finely-kept grounds and called 'The Adelphi Centre.' Here Middleton Murry's community for the study and practice of the new Socialism has been in action for a year. Now the whole house is being surrendered to the family of 29 Basque girls and 24 Basque boys for which the PPU has recently made itself responsible. Before it became the Adelphi Centre

> the name of that house was – and in the locality still is – 'The Oaks'. As you approach it you realise why: for in front of the house and overshadowing the road is one of the most majestic oak trees I have ever seen. So it seems strangely fitting that these little Basques, whose own ancient oak was one of the few things left standing in Guernica, should have come to Langham; and that the house which is to be their temporary home should link in its name the Basque and the English tree.

After the Basque children were found new homes, it became a temporary sanctuary for elderly evacuees from London's East End, before reverting to a second, even less successful attempt at farming.

Yet despite many difficulties, The Adelphi Centre had its triumphs. An annual summer school had been established where the great issues of the day could be discussed. The first was held in Glossop in Derbyshire in 1934, principally aimed at members of the Independent Labour Party in that region, with a mixture of working-class and middle-class supporters attending. 'That experience of mutual discovery,' Murry later wrote, 'is, and always will be, vivid in my memory.' This was followed up a year later at Caerleon, and finally and most famously, the 1936 colloquium held at Langham which included Jack Common, George Orwell, John Macmurray, Reinhold Niebuhr, Karl Polyani, Herbert Read and John Strachey. For what was described as being a place for the cultivation of a new generation of socialists, the colloquium had a decidedly religious inflection. According to the novelist Rayner Heppenstall who attended (and also cooked for it), the Christian philosopher John Macmurray 'dominated the 1936 Summer School', a judgement with which Murry's biographer Frank Lea fully concurred. Macmurray was the coming man.

The summer school ran from 1 to 28 August 1936, with the main lectures held each Saturday and introduced by Murry. George Orwell gave his talk on 4 August under the title 'An Outsider Sees the Distressed Areas', chaired by Rayner Heppenstall. Though Orwell might well have felt uncomfortable with some of the other speakers or people attending, in respect of their pacifist and New Life sympathies – since it was reported that while working in Burma he famously used to tie copies of the more egregious copies of *The Adelphi* to a tree for target practice – he later told his friend Jack Common 'that he enjoyed his visit and met some interesting people and wished he could have stayed longer'. Though Orwell was not a great fan of Murry, the fact is that *The Adelphi* had published one of Orwell's most famous essays, 'A Hanging', in August 1931, and according to biographer D.J. Taylor, Orwell found Richard Rees and Max Plowman 'congenial companions, keeping up with them (Plowman died in 1941) for the rest of his life'. Common's own talk was given under the provocative title 'A Proletarian Theology'.

A strict Protestant who ended life as a Quaker, John Macmurray's mixture of Christian caritas and social gospel was at this juncture compelling. Interest in Macmurray's work is on the rise again amongst communitarians on the right and left. Once described as 'the best-kept secret of twentieth-century British philosophy', Macmurray died in 1976, relatively unknown outside academia until his name resurfaced in the headlines during the early days of the 1997 Labour Government. In an interview with the new Prime Minister, Tony Blair announced that one of the great influences on his life had been his 'favourite philosopher', John Macmurray. It was suggested that Macmurray's precept that 'human life is inherently a common life' was going to be central to the New Labour project, and Blair himself had contributed an enthusiastic foreword to a new anthology of Macmurray's essays published in 1996, a year before the general election which brought him to power. I was intrigued at the time to see where this would lead, but Labour's flirtation with communitarianism did not last long.

Macmurray, like Max Plowman, had fought in the First World War, was badly wounded at Arras, and subsequently awarded the Military Cross. They also shared something else in common: both had been brought up in the austere culture of the Plymouth Brethren, a strict nonconformist sect. Macmurray came back from the war, like so many others, a changed man. In the words of his biographer John E. Costello, 'He had seen howitzers and machine-guns anonymously translate thousands of living men into cannon fodder.' 'We went to war in a blaze of idealism,' Macmurray later wrote,' but by the end of the war we soldiers had largely lost faith in the society we had been fighting for.' He had entered Balliol College in Oxford in 1913 – then 'the centre of liberal theology and democratic socialist thinking in Britain', according to Costello – but his education was disrupted by the war.

Balliol had been a gathering place for philosophers in the Christian socialist tradition, in which the Settlement movement had played an important role. The settlements were outposts of good works in the poorest neighbourhoods in the major cities, places where privileged students could learn about social conditions but also actively endeavour to help change them. In themselves they were communitarian initiatives, with monastic antecedents. At the heart of Macmurray's philosophy, and that of other like-minded philosophical idealists, was the belief that 'Human freedom can be realised only as the freedom of individuals in relation; and the freedom of each of us is relative to that of others.'

Despite his distinguished military record, Macmurray caused controversy when in 1917 he was asked to give a sermon in a London church, and preached reconciliation with the

John Macmurray and John Middleton Murry in conversation at the famous Adelphi Summer School, 1936, on the terrace of The Oaks.

enemy. This did not go down well. In response to the public uproar that ensued, Macmurray resolved that while still a Christian, he would not join any formal church organisation, instead emphasising the primacy of the individual conscience. He later became a popular lecturer on BBC Radio discussing issues of philosophy, religion and ethics. Were it not for his faith, he often told friends, he would be a pessimist. His wife Betty pulled in other directions, deeply sceptical about the world of academia and its relationship to questions of faith and integrity. She was fond of saying that 'Cambridge produced Reformers, Oxford burned them.'

Once described by Arthur Schlesinger as 'the most influential American theologian of the twentieth century', the already distinguished pastor Reinhold Niebuhr also attended the summer school in 1936. A socialist and a pacifist in his early days, he became more pragmatic as he got older but nevertheless was regarded as a formidably articulate defender of liberal values and an elder statesman of the American democratic left. Martin Luther King Jnr was one of his most steadfast admirers, but there were countless others. There on the platform too was another international star, Karl Polyani, whose talk was ambitiously called 'The Nature of the Present World Crisis'. Born into a German-speaking Jewish family in Hungary, Polyani moved to Vienna at the end of the First World War, where he converted to Protestantism. A social democrat and Christian thereafter, he moved to London in 1934 and became close to a number of influential Christian socialists and left-wing intellectuals in Britain, including R.H. Tawney and G.D.H. Cole. Famous for one major work on economics, *The Great Transformation* published in 1944, Polyani died in 1964. To have three intellectual giants of the age present together in a small Essex village was no small achievement, though their names would have been familiar to those like Murry, Plowman, Orwell, Brittain and Watson, all of whom would have encountered their writings in *The Adelphi*. Even Max Plowman, initially sceptical about this kind of gathering, agreed it had gone well.

Another initiative whose impact went beyond the Centre itself and continued throughout the war was the setting up of The Adelphi Players by Richard Ward in 1941, following an article he had written in *The Adelphi* called 'Theatre of Persons'. In a history of radical theatre in this period *Theatres of Conscience*, historian Peter Billingham cites one of The Adelphi Players, John Headley, recalling:

> We started off in a very simple way, just eight of us; I think that there were five men and three women. We started with The Little Plays of St Francis (Housman) and we started off in the summer of 1941, touring around Essex by road, carrying our simple props and travelling by bus and train to the villages and churches of Essex.

The Langham plays had mixed reviews. One of those who attended one of the productions was Trevor Howard, farming nearby, and soon to become intensely involved with Langham and Frating. In a letter to Enid Whitmore, whom he was shortly to marry, dated 4 October 1942, Howard wrote: 'The play at Langham was poor I thought, tho' it was quite well acted. Richard Ward was very charming as Don Juan but the play seemed to have no theme: it didn't hang together. I go to a WEA class every Friday on "Russia" given by an old Girtonian and communist, we have quite fun especially at question time.'

Iris Murdoch was another contributor to *The Adelphi* during the war. She had written about Berdyaev and on current movements in radical Christianity, and in her 1958 novel *The Bell* explored many of the difficulties and fraught relationships involved in communal living. Is it just a coincidence that one of Iris Murdoch's best novels is set in a religious retreat? The novelist and philosopher would have known of The Adelphi Centre through her connections with *The Adelphi*. Murdoch's insights into the potentially disruptive nature of communal living are discussed later, but her personal involvement with Marxism, existentialism and the bohemian world of life and letters, as well as her closeness to some of the editors and contributors of *The Adelphi* in this period, would have kept her in close touch with the growing interest in the communitarian movement.

However, Murry's mind was often elsewhere. He continued to yearn for community, and for him the quintessential model was a proper working farm. 'I wanted to have a hand in the establishment of one. I wanted it to be a farm, because of my deep feeling that in the last resort the whole of civilisation depends on primary production from the land. It is as simple as that.' He had chosen, he recorded later, to go to East Anglia, because 'it is the great home of arable farming'. Though The Adelphi Centre had not been that ideal farm, it had been a first step, and while essentially a political education centre, there had always been a food cultivation element to it and its programme proselytised agricultural self-sufficiency. In Joe Watson's words, 'The Centre was a kind of rallying point for those engaged in establishing land communities.'

Late in the day, a new figure emerged from the records and memories of those involved with the Langham and Frating projects. This was Frank Lea, writer, literary critic, philosopher and poet, a man of enormous erudition and charm according to many, today lost to the literary and political record. 'Our Frank Lea,' Joe Watson always called him. Lea comes and goes at Langham and Frating, though he never stays, but is frequently mentioned with affection. Between 1943 and 1962 he published more than a dozen studies in religion, philosophy and literary criticism, starting with a biography of Carlyle issued in 1943 and finishing with an overview of English romantic poetry, *Voices in the Wilderness*, published in 1975 two years before he took his own life. In between came biographies of Shelley, G.K. Chesterton, John Middleton Murry and Nietzsche, a work on contemporary religious belief, *The Seed of the Church*, a critique of logical positivism, *A Defence of Philosophy*, and several other substantial studies. It seems from these books that Lea could translate from the French and German, and was familiar with all the major schools of philosophy, including the most recent work of the leading European theologians. In Frank Lea both the Langham and Frating projects had their own philosopher to help guide them through the thickets of belief and understanding, with Joe Watson a keen admirer and close friend.

In *A Defence of Philosophy* Lea roundly attacked the Anglo-Saxon school of linguistic analysis, then the most powerful set of ideas in academic philosophy. This was a school of thought preoccupied with the meanings of words and grammatical structures as constituting the essential means of understanding how we discuss and interpret real-life events. Lea wished to return to the original task of philosophy: not to ask what things mean, but rather 'What should be done?' He was in favour of the questions being asked by the European existentialists he and some of theothers of *The Adelphi* circle were reading – Berdyaev, Karl Jaspers, Gabriel Marcel, as well as Macmurray – exploring how we choose to live most meaningfully with the (sometimes limited) freedom we have. Another way of putting this, Lea argued, was to revisit Hume's work, where the key question in moral philosophy remains: how do we move from 'is' to 'ought', or from description to prescription, in pursuit of the ethical life?

Central to these existential arguments about ethics was the vital importance of interpersonal relationships, and in what context these might best flourish. Hence the preoccupation with the notion of 'community', a word that seems to appear in every other sentence written by Murry, Watson and Macmurray, as well as many others associated with 'New Life' ethics. But the word itself is not without its complexities and indeed contradictions, as the critic Raymond Williams has written in his celebrated analysis of 'keywords' in the social and political lexicon:

> Community can be the warmly persuasive word to describe an existing set of relationships, or the warmly persuasive word to describe an alternative set of relationships. What is most important, perhaps, is that unlike all other terms of social organisation (state, nation, society, etc) it seems never to be used unfavourably, and never to be given any positive opposing or distinguishing term.

In short, since nobody can be against community, what does it really mean? For Murry's generation it still retained some of the religious associations of communion, congregation and the monastic tradition. It is not simply shared beliefs or values but shared activity, echoing Macmurray's belief that 'action, not thinking, is the primary and most inclusive domain of human reason in its expression'. From this Macmurray asserts that 'religious truths are verifiable only in living by them within community'. Here, as with Murry on each and every occasion, the word community is never used as an abstract noun denoting a term of social organisation – to cite Williams' phrase – but denotes an ongoing process or state of being. People are not in the community but in community.

Lea's long-standing interest in Nietzsche – then as now a difficult subject, perhaps less so then, before German and Italian fascism claimed him as an inspiration – arises out of his interest in the German philosopher's espousal of the experimental life. Concluding *A Defence of Philosophy*, Lea records Nietzsche's views on this, translated by Lea from the original German: 'Thus we live in a *prospective* or *retrospective* existence, according to our tastes and talents, and the best we can do in this interregnum is to be as much as possible our own *reges* and found little *experimental states*.' This is the Nietzsche that Joe Watson was also reading.

Sceptical of Soviet Russia's claim to be in the process of building a new society which when complete would fulfil the promise of history and culminate in the perfect society, Lea preferred seeing political change as a work in progress that could be modified and adapted as it proceeded, one step at a time. On the matter of final destinations in history, Lea cited a colleague's remark that 'it is a sign of maturity to be able to live with an unfinished world-view'. Elsewhere he joked that the reason why some Soviet philosophers refused to accept the Second Law of Thermodynamics was that it would imply that even a communist utopia would eventually decay. History would then do what Walter Benjamin thought it always did, carry on piling up the rubbish.

The move from Langham

As was now obvious, the self-sufficiency element of The Adelphi Centre had clearly failed, and for Murry the experience was wholly 'disenchanting'. The Basque refugee children had left in 1939, to be replaced by East End evacuees, and when some of those left Plowman tried once again to make it a community project, using the services of the Peace Pledge Union to recruit a number of young pacifists to renovate the house and commence farming again. It was known as the Farm Group, Murry's son Colin later wrote of it that 'The laudable aim of the Group was to pay their own way and, as far as I could make out, in pursuit of this aim they subsisted almost entirely on a diet of lentils, porridge and milk. On my first visit to the cottage (inhabited by the Farm Group) I found myself being reminded irresistibly of Cold Comfort Farm.'

By this time Trevor Howard was becoming more involved with Langham and went to stay there from time to time 'to sample community life'. In another letter to Enid Whitmore he wrote that:

> I'm sleeping in No.14 with 5 others so that it seems like going back to school again. In the next bed is Dan suffering from Rheumatoid Arthritis which has almost paralysed him (he's an evacuee) and when he arrived to bed at 8.45 I simply didn't dare pity myself any longer. 'I never thought I should get in this mess,' he said, 'still you never know your luck and there are thousands worse – life is still sweet.' I felt so terribly sorry. We chatted away and he seemed to have got hold of the idea of triumph thro' suffering and to draw, if not comfort at any rate patience from it.

The Peace Pledge Union camp at Swanwick in 1937. In the front row from left to right: the man in the dark jacket, spectacles, and open shirt is James Whitmore, father of Enid Howard (née Whitmore) and grandfather of Katherine Weaver (née Howard), then his wife Mary Whitmore, then John Middleton Murray and then Dick Sheppard. Max Plowman, wearing a dark tie and suit, is the sixth person to the left of James Whitmore.

Vera Brittain came to Langham on several occasions towards the end and it left a great impression on her, for good and bad. She and husband George Catlin had sent their two children to America for the duration of the war, while she carried on campaigning. It could not have been a happy time for Brittain: without her children, scorned in the press and with Britain now at war, its major cities sustaining heavy bombing from the air resulting in many casualties and much destruction. Even so, her impressions are acute and memorable. In *Testament of Experience* she described life at The Adelphi Centre as 'a bit like living in a monastery, very simple and lacking in heating'. She was no admirer of Murry's regime either: 'a massive *Herrenvolk* with an auxiliary chorus of women'. The anarchist writer George Woodcock, who had visited, stayed for a short while and then hurriedly left to go to another farm, was even less impressed:

> When I went to Langham, I thought I might enter wholly into the community pattern of living and stay for a long time, perhaps for the duration of the war, as a kind of lay monk in a model of an ideal society. I stayed only a few months; it was a period of hope and disillusionment, of joy mingled with frustration, of intense new friendships which did not last and of bewildering hostilities with people whose ideals and aims I shared.

Woodcock went on to detail the problem in terms of the competing beliefs and value systems evident there:

> Under the same roof were anarchists, left-wing socialists and secular-minded pacifists; there were Quakers, Plymouth Brethren, Catholics and one mild-mannered man who professed himself a Satanist; there were vegetarians, bicycle-club enthusiasts, esperantists and nudists.

Yet when Murry was absent, Brittain remembers Langham fondly, particularly after her bruising experiences in the public arena. 'Here I stayed for long periods,' she recalled, 'caring for the evacuees and tending the garden,' she later wrote, 'and found a healing contentment in the open country, reminiscent of Holland, where pageants of cloud marched over the wide horizons and wild flowers filled the lanes with their blue and yellow.'

Many years later, in another letter written by Trevor Howard but this time to his daughter Katherine, he likened the Farm Group to 'Snow White and the Seven Dwarfs'. Only one person knew anything about farming, wrote Howard, himself a farmer. 'Geoff Phillips was in charge, a strange forceful frustrated young man who knew a little about farming, which none of the others did. There was Peter Wells, the Barrett brothers, Frank Lea for a time and so on and Murry coming down at weekends and telling them to go in for "low living and high thinking".' The Farm Group's attempts failed yet again, by which time Murry realised that supporting eight or nine people on 70 acres of neglected land with little or no capital could never be viable, even for the most experienced farm manager.

There was actually one other visitor to Langham who had farming experience: Hugh Barrett. He later farmed professionally for several decades before going on to work in international development and education, eventually writing two evocative memoirs about traditional farming in Suffolk, *Early to Rise*, published in 1967 and *A Good Living*, published in 2000. Born in Colchester in 1917, as a young man Barrett had undertaken a farming pupillage. In 1939, having helped his father at a camp established for Jewish refugee children at Dovercourt, near Harwich, he came to meet some of those associated with the Langham project, who had also been involved with supporting Basque and

Jewish refugees. In *A Good Living* he recalled that 'For some months I had whenever possible gone down for weekends to a pacifist community of mostly young people living in a large Edwardian house at Langham near Colchester, and I had fallen in love with Deirdre, a girl who was living there and who soon became my wife.'

In a final attempt to rescue the project, in 1941 Murry invited his long-standing acolyte Joe Watson to come to Langham as manager, which the latter was more than happy to do. Watson's son Peter later recalled that 'When Max Plowman gave up the wardenship of Langham, Murry asked my father to take his place. "It was," my mother once told me, "as if God himself had commanded him."' Joe Watson remembered much the same feelings:

> I had been keen on the idea of the Centre from the beginning, and suggested I should join and do what I could to help. There was little scope for me at the time (when Watson first attended the 1936 summer school), but in 1941 Max Plowman died suddenly, and I was asked to be Warden in the emergency. After 14 years at blast-furnaces this was a challenge indeed, and without any more ado, I packed up and with wife and two children arrived with the exciting project of working immediately with Murry in something he really wanted to do.

Plowman died of pneumonia in June 1941 at Langham, where he is buried, though he had already set in train plans to establish yet another communal farm for conscientious objectors, set in 300 acres at Holton-cum-Beckering in Lincolnshire. We know more about this modest community because it was where the parents of actor Jim Broadbent settled, one a sculptor, the other a furniture-maker. Both were pacifists. The links between Langham and Holton were convivial: in a letter from Trevor Howard to Enid in October

1942, Howard writes that 'Joe and Cynthia [Copnall] have gone to Holton Beckering for the Harvest Festival.' Plowman had been loved and admired by many who came into contact with him, but he had his weaknesses, as the same people also admitted. Vera Brittain, who got to know him well during her times at The Adelphi Centre, was one such person. She liked Plowman but said of him that he was 'organisationally incompetent to a degree'.

It didn't take very long for Murry and Watson to have differences over the way forward and the two subsequently agreed to go separate ways. Reading the letters from Murry to Watson in this period, still in the possession of Watson's family, it is clear that Murry was desperate for someone to come and rescue him from the disorganisation at Langham, and basically, as soon as Watson arrived, Murry retreated, leaving Watson to clear up the mess. Watson would have been invited earlier, but privately both Plowman and Murry agreed that the situation then at Langham was no place for a conventional family with young children, and so delayed the invitation to the very last. When the Air Ministry decided to requisition the house and land for a new airfield, Watson realised that 'The time was ripe for us to part and he [Murry] went off with a group of young men to found a communal farm and I was left to pick up the bits and wind the affairs of the Centre up.' In 1943 – the Air Ministry having now decided against its purchase – The Oaks was sold on to Essex County Council, where it became a school for students with special needs. Renamed 'The Homestead', today it continues catering for young people with special educational needs.

In addition to Joe Watson's enthusiasm for a fresh start, Hugh Barrett's interest was also quickened by the prospect of a new project, especially when asked to become farm manager on the basis of his prior experience:

> It was decided to buy a farm and work it communally and after a short search they found a very suitable three hundred acres with a large house and four cottages – enough to house as many as were likely to want an agricultural life. Deirdre was among them and when it was suggested and voted I should join them as farm manager, I agreed to throw in my lot.

In a letter from Joe to Hugh Barrett on 25 May 1942, Joe gathered his core group together: 'You and Roderic, and Roy Butcher and Deirdre, Jane and Greta, all so precious to me… Between us we will move mountains.' At this time they were looking at a farm at Ashdon, near Saffron Walden, 140 acres of boulder clay, but within two months they discovered Frating, much better by far. In his diary Hugh Barrett records on Monday 17 August 1942: 'Joe goes to see Sexton with T [Trevor Howard] & J.P. [John Plowright]. Hot weather good: routine jobs. I should ring Joe tonight. Swim with Simon Bennett. Canoe on river.' Two days later Barrett was still thinking about the offer of becoming farm manager at Frating: 'Write to Joe expressing feeling about the job of managing and rather doubtful about things.' Hugh Barrett's energy and experience were, one suspects, key to the successful move to Frating, though his doubts remained, and once there and settled in with Deirdre, within a year he decided to move on.

Once the decision to go separate ways was agreed between Murry and Watson, Murry moved fast, buying a farm on the Suffolk–Norfolk border. On 13 April 1942, he wrote in his diary:

> I have paid the deposit on the farm, which I am buying for £3,325. Buying it and capitalizing it will take, quite literally, every penny I possess: so much at least and possibly more. I suppose it's a great risk.

> My one regret is that I am 52, nearly 53, and a semi-invalid. I would give a good deal for a sound pair of legs. But one can't have everything: and if I last out 10 more years – having had a hand in creating one of the elements of a new society – I shan't have done badly.

Thus in October 1942, Murry left Langham to set up another communal farm for conscientious objectors at Lodge Farm in Thelnetham, while Watson and Barrett left some months later to establish a new pacifist communal farm in Frating, a tiny hamlet east of Colchester in Essex, where Frating Hall Farm was up for rent or sale.

In those days it appears the buying and selling of farms was commonplace, and occupation a moveable feast. Murry records the transference of goods, not including livestock, from Langham to Thelnetham as requiring twelve return journeys by lorry, carrying:

> Adelphi cottage furniture
> Ditto
> 3 tons carrots
> Horse Rake and Ploughs
> Wagon and Horse-hoe
> Binder
> Tumbril and Roll
> Tumbril and Tanks
> Tiles and Timber
> Corn
> Furniture, Stoves, etc
> Seed Potatoes, Wire Netting, etc

Three cows, five heifers, twenty ewes and four horses went separately. Both men felt bad about the divisive last days at Langham and made peace to some extent through later correspondence. Novelist Rayner Heppenstall recalls that it was Watson 'who threw the first handful of earth into Murry's grave' at the latter's funeral in 1957. Watson's wife Doris, however, never approved of Murry, for as their younger daughter Jan recalled, 'My mother was horrified that Murry had all these women, because that wasn't what you did if you came from Consett!'

Among those who went with Watson, his wife Doris and their two children, were Trevor Howard, Hugh Barrett, Roderic Barrett, together with his wife Lorna, Deirdre Crosfield, Donald and Doreen Whitehouse, Irene Palmer and Peter Wells, the last a conscientious objector who had recently served a short term of hard labour in Norwich Prison for his beliefs. Soon after, Trevor was joined by Enid Whitmore whom he married once he had settled at Frating. The small party set off in high hopes, embarking in Joe Watson's words 'on a journey to our heart's desire'.

4. Bread salted with tears

> What stands fast in the English countryside today? Primarily, and almost solely, the duty towards the land.
>
> JOHN MIDDLETON MURRY, *Community Farm*

Pioneers, Oh Pioneers!

According to Donald Whitehouse, by December 1943 the small party which left Langham for Frating had grown considerably: 'there were thirty people in our community, including seven married couples and seven children – with Grandad Evans, from the Oaks, representing the other end of the generations'. By 1948 the community was made up of 'nine married couples with fifteen children between them, living in houses and cottages, and ten single men and women living in the Hall'. At its busiest Frating Hall Farm was a home to more than forty permanent residents, and these numbers were complemented by visitors arriving and staying to help at harvest time. From time to time the farm also provided shelter and work for some European refugees, and several prisoners-of-war. Thus at any one time there may have been more than fifty people living at Frating Hall Farm.

Trevor Howard recalled the momentous occasion in a letter to his daughter Katherine, written some years after, in 1962:

> At our last Sunday at The Oaks we had a sort of dedication service and Joe read Noah's sailing in the Ark – it sounds comical in retrospect but it was

> strangely impressive at the time. Those first days at Frating were terrific, you got a marvellous sense of freedom when you have abandoned all your possessions and get a wonderful sense of togetherness – of working together, of sharing together and coming together in the evenings to sing and talk and tell funny stories and recount the day's doings with a bit of embroidery – a gorgeous feeling of losing oneself in the mass, the community, the movement.

Howard played a vital role in these early days, since along with Hugh Barrett he was the only other one with farming experience. His father Harry Howard had been badly gassed during the First World War, and was subsequently trained in fruit farming as part of a government rehabilitation scheme. Trevor was born in Lincolnshire in 1919, and became a pacifist at school, after reading of the horrors of the First World War. As a young reader of *Peace News*, like so many others he fell under the spell of Dick Sheppard. In 1938 Howard passed the entrance exam for Pembroke College, Cambridge, and as soon as he got to university he joined the Fellowship of Reconciliation, a Christian pacifist organisation. On receiving his call-up papers in 1939, Howard applied to the Cambridge Local Tribunal to be registered as a conscientious objector. The following year his father Harry bought 'Lufkins', a small mixed farm of 23 acres at Dedham, close to Langham, putting Trevor in charge. Whether this was a way of reconciling his son's beliefs with the legitimate claims of those working in farming to be exempted from military service, we can only guess. Once at Lufkins Howard soon became involved in the activities of The Adelphi Centre, and thus got to know and admire Murry, Plowman and Watson and what they were doing.

In the same letter to Katherine, Howard specifically

mentions that as far as he was concerned, the Frating experiment had its idealistic origins in that early attempt by Murry and D.H. Lawrence to create a model community during the First World War mentioned at the outset, recording that:

> At a time of turmoil when the failure of the old form and patterns of society are shown up in their true light there is a need to try something new – to experiment. An older root in Frating's case – because Frating was really born at Langham 'Oaks' and Langham had started before the war as a community under the inspiration of Middleton Murry, and going back to D.H. Lawrence (you remember in Lawrence's Letters, his wanting to start a community with Murry and one or two like-minded folk way back 1914–1918).

It was around this time that Howard met Enid Whitmore at a discussion group organised by a local postmaster in neighbouring East Bergholt – where Howard's parents lived – to which guest speakers were invited. In the summer of 1942, the speaker was Mrs Mary Whitmore, a well-known and formidable pacifist and feminist. She went home and told her daughter about the young farmer at Dedham. Meeting shortly after, they fell in love and married a year later: the first marriage to be celebrated at Frating. Their daughter Katherine kept their letters to each other, from which we know that in October 1942 Howard wrote to Enid:

> After milking I offs to Langham, had supper with Joe and said, 'What do you think's a good time to get married?' 'Any time' he said, 'sooner the better.' 'There is,' I said, 'a coldness in the older generation.' 'Ah!' he said, waxing serious. 'Something went dead in that generation.' And suggested we must not allow the dead hand to kill the life within us.

Not content with this advice, Howard asked further:

> This afternoon I went to Colchester and went down to tea with Cecil Barrett – the old Quaker bloke – 'what do you think about it?' I said. 'I don't think 19 is too young' he said, 'my eldest boy married a 19-year-old girl – her people were a little opposed at first but they soon came round. Love and youth and joy are not things to be kept waiting or suppressed they are tender plants and mustn't be frustrated.

Enid was born in 1923, the only child of two teachers. Her mother, Mary Whitmore, weathered her reputation as a feminist to eventually became the first Lady Mayor of Ipswich. Enid's father had, like Plowman and Macmurray themselves, fought in the First World War, and likewise the experience had made him become a pacifist. When she first met Howard, she had been a student at King's College, London (though at that point the college had been evacuated to Bristol). Enid therefore had to make the decision to abandon her studies to join her future husband in the farm project, aware that the marriage was strongly opposed by both sets of parents. Enid was then only nineteen, and legally a minor, and could have been prevented from marrying by application to the courts. Nevertheless, the marriage went ahead, and lasted until Trevor's death in 2002, fifty-seven years later. Enid died in 2016, her funeral attended by many former Frating members, including Shirley Williams, of whom we shall hear more.

In the early days at Frating, Enid and Trevor shared a cottage with another newly married couple, Roderic and Lorna Barrett, an arrangement that proved difficult since it involved Trevor and Enid having 'to climb to their bedroom using a chair on a table and a hole in the ceiling to avoid having to go through Roderic and Lorna's bedroom'. Roderic Barrett and his older brother Hugh had both been involved with The Adelphi Centre. Their father, a Congregationalist before becoming a Quaker – and the man who gave Trevor the advice on the joys of early marriage – had been imprisoned during the First World War as a conscientious objector, and both sons followed suit in adopting pacifist beliefs. Though Hugh had been asked to take on the job of farm manager at Frating, once he had met Deirdre at Langham and they decided to become a couple, they didn't stay long. He found the inexperience of others, and their assumptions of what farm work involved, difficult to accept, though he was in no doubt as to their good intentions.

> In no way I regret taking on that job. It taught me a lot about myself and how community living, so attractive in theory, can become very emotionally tangled and unhappy. I knew, although I liked and admired many members of the community and the farm was a fine and productive one, that this was not my scene. Nor was Deirdre comfortable in this situation, so the decision to leave was easy.

Hugh Barrett went on to farm in Suffolk for several decades before taking up work in Africa in the field of international development and education. He and Deirdre remained married for over fifty years until her death in 1997. Deirdre was already a kindred spirit. She was born in Canada, and her parents had moved to England at the outbreak of the First World War so that her father could enlist here. In the 1930s she had voluntarily worked with the unemployed in Durham and in fact may have met Joe Watson there at the time. She then worked in London's East End during the Blitz with a group of conscientious objectors, before arriving at Frating in 1944 and falling in love with Hugh. A lifelong artist, her botanical drawings are now in the collection at Kew Gardens.

In addition to becoming a well-known broadcaster on farming matters for the BBC, towards the end of his life

Hugh Barrett became closely involved with the international Campaign Against the Arms Trade, continuing the beliefs of his own father. Hugh was another of those who most definitely had mixed feelings about Murry. He thought Murry's books and lectures were wonderful, but 'I disliked him intensely... the meanest man on earth.' He was not the only one who found Murry obsessive about money – a common complaint throughout Murry's life. Ironically, it was almost certainly because Murry was often the only one with significant amounts of money, invariably invested in all his Quixotic ventures, and consequently its security was often the overriding matter on his mind.

Roderic and Lorna Barrett had their first child at Frating: Jonathan Barrett was born there in 1944. Roderic had been something of a child prodigy, in 1935 managing to secure a place at the Central School of Art and Design in London at the age of fifteen. He left the Central School in 1940, having studied under William Roberts and Bernard Meninsky. Roderic appears to have found a role at Frating by being designated as the 'resident artist', according to his biographer David Buckman, but later admitted that 'I was absolutely a fish out of water, the wrong material altogether.' Roderic and Lorna were eventually asked to leave, a cause of great distress to Roderic at the time and for some time after, though Lorna on the other hand apparently found leaving Frating 'very, very hard, because I loved the place and it was ideal for children'. Roderic agreed that Lorna felt very differently to him on this matter, later saying that Lorna 'had been very happy at Frating. She is basically a pioneer, someone who would have been suited if she had set out into the wilderness and built her own cabin.' Alas, Roderic was not cut from the same cloth. This was an early sign that the different experiences of men, women and children in their time at Frating Hall were considerable, ranging from the traumatic to the idyllic.

These differences form an important part of the story as their testimonies confirm, though whether the wider world offers anything more amenable to the differing needs and interests of women and men remains open to question.

Nevertheless, after leaving Frating, Roderic Barrett found national recognition as an artist, going on to play an important part in the artistic life of the county and beyond. With Cedric Morris, Lett Haines and John Nash, he helped establish the Colchester Art Society and was a central figure in the rich artistic milieu which developed around the Essex–Suffolk border at this time. This important artistic revival had its origins in the time when Cedric Morris first established the East Anglian School of Painting and Drawing in 1937 at Dedham, just two miles from Langham (where Lucien Pissarro, brother-in-law of Samuel Bensusan, was often to be found, living next door to The Adelphi Centre), before moving to Benton End in Hadleigh, Suffolk, after the war. This was where Morris and his partner Lett Haines established a small residential art college that in a very short time gained a considerable reputation, not only as a bohemian enclave but as a forcing house of genuine artistic achievement, with students such as Maggi Hambling amongst its number. This was a time when many artists took an active interest in international affairs, helping practically when they could. At Great Bardfield in Essex, not too far away, painter Edward Bawden had opened his home to several officers from the defeated Republican side in the Spanish Civil War, as well as Jewish refugees.

Bread salted with tears

In retrospect one person appears to have dominated the proceedings of the Frating Hall community, and that was Joe Watson, who had led the exodus from Langham. His vision and energy proved critical – even if at times disruptive. This

From left to right: Deirdre Barrett, John Barrett, Joe Watson, Ruth Barrett, Doris Watson, Oliver Barnard, Frank Lea. Taken circa 1957 at Street Farm, Great Glenham, Suffolk.

has always been acknowledged by other members, even those who disagreed him at times. Some of this may stem from the fact that he was older than most of the others and may have acted as a father figure, if not a prophet leading a small tribe out of the wilderness. Watson was 41 in 1943, Trevor Howard, 24, Enid Whitmore, 20, Hugh Barrett, 26, Roderic Barrett, 23. Also unusual perhaps was that Joe Watson was a man who had an extremely tough upbringing, who was a socialist, and yet who was in no way a class warrior, nor, despite his profound Christian beliefs, a religious zealot. There is nothing in his writings that rages against class enemies, denounces high finance or boardroom impropriety, attacks parliamentary privilege or calls for revolution. Nor does he denounce the Anglican establishment, or engage in religious sectarianism. He is simply for 'Life'.

In addition, Joe was married and had children. He and his wife Doris had met and married in Consett, having their first daughter Joan in 1932, Janice in 1939 and finally son Peter in 1945. It seems that like Joe, Doris had become something of a parental figure at Langham, with Trevor Howard describing her in a letter as 'a very good soul, kind, sure, capable, alive but very deaf'. An accomplished dressmaker she offered to make Trevor and Enid's wedding dress. Joe worried that some of the younger, more educated women at Langham 'think Doris less than she is', and admitted that he himself sometimes 'takes her for granted while her deafness is a genuine barrier for one cannot shout the things one must only whisper', he wrote with a delicate turn of phrase. But in many ways, he was acutely dependent on her for support.

Unusual too was his status in the group that went to Frating. It was a reverse image of how authority in the armed services operated. Here was someone who had left school at twelve, now leading a group of highly educated earnest young religious idealists, quite the opposite of how authority worked in military life, where it was invariably highly educated upper-class officers who commanded squads of poorly educated recruits. The fact is that his personality enlarged the lives of everybody he met, and even if some of those closest to him at Frating grew disillusioned with his charismatic character at times, it is doubtful whether the experiment would have lasted quite so long without him. In a letter from Middleton Murry to Joe in 1941, the former just having visited the new pacifist community at Holton-cum-Beckering, Murry attributes the happy atmosphere there to the fact that 'they have a good father figure, which the Langham lads lack'. For a while Frating had just such a father figure, with all the positive – and occasionally difficult outcomes – such a position would produce.

Watson's robust personality had been tempered in the harshness of a childhood lived in poverty and family tragedy in Consett. He was the second-eldest of ten children, whose parents both died within months of each other in their forties, requiring six of the children to be separated and taken in care. Joe was seventeen when this happened but he had already been at work for five years. 'He took the Labour Exam at school when he was twelve,' his younger daughter Jan told me, 'and if you passed you were allowed to go out to work. We've got his certificate still.' Joe and his older brother stayed in the family home and looked after two other older children, while the six younger ones were split up and assigned to children's homes many miles from each other. His bitterness at the cruelty of enforced family separation lasted a lifetime. One day during a visit to Derbyshire, Jan suggested a trip to Ashbourne in the Peak District. Joe replied, 'I don't want to go there – that's where your Aunt Ethel was incarcerated in a children's home!' As a result, all the siblings became very family-oriented, Jan told me, 'though I think my father was the only one who was a socialist'.

Joe also gained his strength and resilience from a rich ply of Anglican conscience, Lawrentian vitalism and a steadfast conviction that 'fellowship is life'. This last sentiment was the creed of the socialist Clarion Cycling Club to which Joe Watson had belonged in his Consett days. In the balance of these forces one predominated. When I asked Jan which had been most important to him, Christianity or socialism, she replied instantly: 'Christianity by far!' His Christianity was elemental, citing approvingly a remark by Havelock Ellis that 'The man who cannot sing while carrying his cross had better drop it.' Jan told me that as a pacifist during the First World War in Consett he had on occasion been given a white feather, the ultimate act of humiliation exacted upon those who refused to fight, and one which was indeed a cross to bear.

In a memoir of his childhood upbringing at Frating, Joe's son Peter wrote that:

> My father was in his early forties and a man of great passion and conviction… He was not content to merely talk or write about it, he felt compelled to demonstrate with his life's work the duty he felt all men owed to humanity to do something positive to change the state of the world. This may sound lofty, and may make my father sound like a fanatic or a dreamer. He was neither. But he did believe in himself, and for most of his life he believed in the power of fellowship.

He was also a man who from past experience was able to put his hand to anything. Sid Chaplin, the former Durham miner described earlier, had known Joe Watson from their early days, a friendship that lasted until Watson's death. In a short introduction to a collection of Watson's writings, Chaplin describes Joe's life in its formative, turbulent years:

> J.H. Watson was born at Wallsend-on-Tyne in 1902 and left school at twelve. He worked as a shop boy, a driver and stableman, a blacksmith's striker and went to sea at the age of sixteen. He fired boilers and worked in the steel-rolling mills at Consett until 1921 and after as a blast-furnace man, with long periods of unemployment.

In a talk he wrote and gave for the BBC in March 1955 under the title 'On Being Hungry', Watson devoted a paragraph to the early days at Frating:

> I was one of a group which tried to create a community. We gathered a lot of money together from all kinds of people, and bought a farm. The farm was to be the sort of foundation stone upon which we built. We were idealistic to the nth degree, we were all of us anxious that we should succeed in creating

> something worthwhile, and to that end we slaved like horses and worked without regard to hours. But an essential part of the scheme was that we should equally share the planning and management of the farm, and so we had a farm meeting each week when everybody aired their views and a policy was hammered out.

These meetings soon became fractious, and were at times ‘horribly contentious occasions’, according to Watson. Remembering from his childhood that family rows were often resolved over tea or the coming together over a meal, Watson inaugurated a weekly farm supper, with the business discussion following the communal meal. Things improved.

Watson told this story in his BBC talk which, time after time, referred back to the breaking of bread, as the key ritual of a sociable life. ‘Bread to me is life, not a thing to exchange for another commodity. I’ve seen my mother’s tears fall into the baking of it.’ This belief was confirmed by his daughter Jan: ‘If my mother had to throw away stale bread (usually given to the pigs) when it was no longer needed, she had to do it when my father wasn’t there. He couldn’t bear it. His reverence for bread was so great he could not bear the thought of it being thrown away because it was, literally, the bread of life.’ This deeply religious approach to food and its origins was evident even in the language of statements he made in what was otherwise an annual company report, asserting that ‘farming is not only work, but the witnessing of a great mystery, the mystery of birth and growth’.

The main cause of early dissatisfaction was not about principles but practical matters. In a short note written by Marian Crosfield in 1951 and clearly intended for circulation amongst other community members, she recorded that:

> The things which are owned collectively are land, machinery, livestock, houses and a farm car, and with the exception of houses, these collectively

> owned things have not been the cause of quarrels and dissatisfaction among members. With regard to houses, inequality of housing is inevitable as some of the cottages owned by the Society are less attractively modern than others and there have been disagreements about who should live in which. The houses are rented to members, usually for a sum of 2/6d or 5/- per week. There is no communal feeding, married members eat in their own home, whilst the Hall accommodates the unmarried men and women.

This situation was fairly late in the day, as at the beginning of the endeavour everyone was suffering from poor accommodation. It is debatable whether this situation was made easier or more difficult by a founding principle that members were accommodated as singles or as married couples (with or without children), but never as cohabiting couples. It is clear that there had been problems at Langham with on/off relationships developed by a fast-changing ensemble of volunteers, and at Frating this potential difficulty was quashed from the start.

Phoebe Lambert arrived at Frating in 1945 at the age of three, with her parents Joanna and Kenneth Lambert, and baby brother. Her parents had met at a Peace Pledge Union meeting, inspired as Brittain and other members of Frating had been by Dick Sheppard. 'I've got my mother's Peace Pledge Union badge,' she told me when I interviewed her in 2019.

> That's where she met my father at the PPU in 1938. My father was only 20 years old and my mother was 30. They were very much in thrall to people like John Middleton Murry. There were other people who certainly influenced my parents' thinking. Dick Sheppard was a very close friend and a big influence on my parents. They admired him greatly. He probably sowed the seeds of their desire to join a pacifist community.

Phoebe Lambert still has some of the letters from Joe Watson discussing whether the Lambert family might be able to join the community, negotiations which carried on for several months. In one letter to Phoebe's father Kenneth, Watson describes the project in uncompromising terms:

> This is the set-up here. We have never had people leave us – we have asked some people to leave because they wished to live out of wedlock. I don't think many schemes can stand this, we cannot. I am not persuaded that it's a good thing in itself. I get tired of hearing lust confused with love. On the other hand, we have had to accept some folk who never really understood what the place was aiming at, and one gets weary waiting for the only spirit which can achieve what we hoped for, the spirit which enables men and women to earn their bread gracefully, orderly, efficiently and without exploitation either economic, moral, spiritual.

He warns of the hard work involved and the possibility of disillusionment. In another letter, dated 3 July 1945, he writes: 'I wouldn't ask my best friend to come into a place like this. It's the biggest job people can ever tackle. But I believe something good can come of it.' Eventually agreement on terms was reached, which included all of the Lambert family's savings – a sum of several thousand pounds acquired through the sale of their Devon smallholding – being invested in shares in the venture. Watson then welcomed the family warmly, while making clear that there was a trial period to see if both parties were happy with the arrangements agreed, as Watson wrote in a concluding letter: 'About you, I want you to get here, and all the family. The meeting agrees with me, on the usual terms, free to leave if you want to after the first four months and us to be free to say we don't want you. It never happens.' This last statement is not quite true of course, as it had happened once before.

For the first few months the Lambert family lived in the 'chitting shed' (where potatoes are stored) before moving to a nearby cottage. Life was hard. Both parents 'worked round the clock', planting potatoes and cabbages, hoeing, muckraking, feeding the chickens, collecting eggs and preparing communal meals. Yet while the adults laboured from dawn to dusk, and occasionally argued about who was or was not pulling their weight, the children found themselves living in arcadia. There were fifteen children at Frating in Lambert's time, free to range the fields, woods and the unmarked lanes that surrounded the settlement's isolated hinterland. If for the adults the going was tough, most of the children felt they had found Eden.

Soon after, in 1946, Derek Crosfield joined the group at Frating, having made initial contact several years earlier with some of its members at Langham. Born in 1915 and educated at Leighton Park School, a boarding school for Quakers, and then Cambridge, he spent some time in the 1930s working at a Quaker Settlement in the Rhondda Valley, which provided relief and support for unemployed miners. He also spent a year as Acting Warden at an educational settlement in the Rhymney Valley. Coming from a Quaker business family, he had experience of management and finance, but for most of the war he was working at an agricultural community in Hampshire: 'It was a small community of half-a-dozen COs and our efforts were at times inexpert. On our eight acres we grew a lot of market gardening crops and kept goats, ducks, geese and hens.' Then came the shocking news that his parents had both been killed and the family home destroyed by a V-1 flying bomb. Now keener than ever on life on the land, he went to Frating, where he met and married Phyllis Marian Thomas, a young widow who had joined Frating in 1945 with her young son Martyn. Crosfield was part of the small group who bought out Frating Hall Farm when the cooperative arrangement came to an end in 1958. As owners of the farm, Derek and Marian stayed at Frating until 1974, after which they moved to Colchester. The title to the farm was then handed on to Martyn Thomas and his family. At Frating Derek had shared Trevor Howard's affection for poultry, and the two remained close friends for the rest of their lives.

5. 'One wants to heal the wounds a little, and help to remake England'

Huge optimism, huge conviviality, and a great sense that anything was possible.

PHOEBE LAMBERT

'Our first weeks at Frating were very memorable,' Trevor Howard wrote in 1946, three years after the advance party took over the farm in March 1943. 'I shall never forget the excitement of the sale, of moving in, and of our first night at the Hall. How we used to sing around the kitchen table in the evenings.' There had originally been just eight members meeting in Joe's study at Langham to plan the move, 'and no one would have guessed that in three years we would number about fifty – I say about fifty, because I can't keep count of the children,' he recalled.

Frating Hall Farm consisted of 300 acres, of which 240 was arable and the rest made up of pasture and permanent woodland. Frating Hall itself is a Grade II listed building, now the long-standing home of Martyn and Barbara Thomas. The 'Hall' as it was always called, consists of a sixteenth-century timber-framed building with eighteenth-and nineteenth-century red-brick facing, and a red-tiled roof. Close by is the main barn dating back to the seventeenth or eighteenth century, an imposing structure of timber uprights, cross-beams, diagonal braces, supporting a tiled roof and clapboard cladding, with a wagon porch on either side. To regard these Essex tithe barns as vernacular cathedrals is not hyperbole,

A young Martyn Thomas watches the unloading of sheaves of corn into the threshing machine at Frating Hall Farm, circa 1950. He is still there today, seventy years later, as part of the family partnership that owns and runs the farm.

and in the life of the Frating Community the barn fulfilled many of the same functions, as theatre, meeting-place, prayer and choir hall, and winter shelter for corn and hay. It was also the final home for *The Adelphi* printing press, according to Peter Watson, which John Middleton Murry tried to recover but to no avail.

At Frating, hall, barn, cottages and outbuildings form the centre of the settlement, with fields stretching out in all directions. A narrow tree-lined drive leads to and from the Hall to the public road, with a beautiful wooden signboard featuring a plough carved by Mark Harvey, announcing Frating Hall Farm at the entrance. At the junction where the farm entrance meets the road stands Frating Church with its small churchyard, the church itself now converted into a private residence. The origins of this small, still pretty twelfth-century church was that it was once a chapel-of-ease to Great Bentley, and originally had a tower with three bells, but this was demolished in 1976 for safety reasons, and the church was subsequently declared redundant.

Unmarried men and women members lived in the Hall. In time seven cottages were made inhabitable or built new for married couples and their children, though in the early days at least one shed and a granary loft were adapted as living accommodation on a temporary basis, while new accommodation was being constructed by the building team. Phoebe Lambert spent nearly all of her childhood at Frating, happily so, though the first days did not start well.

> There was a big problem about accommodation because the Hall could accommodate only so many people. When Joe wrote to my father he said, 'I don't know where to put you.' In the end when we did get to Frating we had a few nights in the Hall and then went to live in what was the chitting shed. I remember well it didn't have a bathroom, just an outside loo, and my brother was born there in 1946 and we were there for seven or eight months. We then moved down to one of the cottages. There were three cottages which Joe had acquired as part of the deal. Then at one point two more houses were built, and we eventually moved out of our tiny cottage into one of the newly built houses.

The money needed to buy Frating Hall Farm was made up of donations by sympathisers to the pacifist cause, of which Vera Brittain was one, supplemented by the savings of would-be members. In addition, the farm's owner, a Mr Sexton, much impressed by Watson's sincerity, helped them raise a mortgage in the region of £6,000 on favourable terms. Janice Smith recalled that:

> The person they purchased the farm from became a lifelong friend of my father. They had nothing in common apart from the fact that they bought the farm from him. About once a month my father would say, 'I must go and see old Sexton,' and he would walk there, quite a long way, and they would chat about life. When the farm folded, Dad was really depressed and Mr Sexton bought him a house and said to him, 'It's your house, and, if you can pay for it then that's alright, but if you can't, then it's a gift.' You'd have to have quite a relationship with somebody if they were willing to give you a house.

As was made clear to Phoebe Lambert's parents, new members had to invest such money as they had in the form of shareholdings in the Frating Hall Farming Society Limited, the company registered under the Industrial and Providential Societies Acts on 24 December 1942, to administer and manage the estate and its business. In December 1943, the year after purchase, the farm, land and associated buildings were valued as fixed assets at just over £8,000; the company also owned Lufkins Farm in Dedham, valued at just £965. From these figures it seems that farms and the land that belonged to them were relatively cheap to buy at this time. But there was a war on, and machinery, livestock and seed corn proved unexpectedly expensive. In addition, there were ongoing overheads for wages, repairs and maintenance. A later note in the Society's minutes confirmed that 'Most of it [the farm machinery] was bought at a time of high prices and doubtful quality – 1942–1946 – which contributed to the high capitalisation of this farm.'

Once again we are lucky to have Trevor Howard's letters to Enid in the early days, as he captures the range of ambitions of the would-be farmers emerging from his record of one of the weekly meetings. Here is an excerpt from his letter dated 1 June 1943:

Tonight should be exciting. It's the meeting and the main discussion is on 'Our aims as a Society' dealing with principles, ideals, purposes, how we are to use the profits. I plan to say we must devote our profits to service – to famine relief after the war – to giving slum children holidays etc. We must not just settle down to be little capitalist farmers making 'our little pile' and living at a high standard in a secure niche, ours is a great and terrible responsibility. In practice, I will say that the one thing we must do is increase our numbers slightly so that each of us gets a little more time to express herself or himself, to do the particular thing he or she wants to do and to run the farm better, so that we don't have to employ casual labour.

Joe opened the discussion and spoke wonderfully well. We had come together, he said, driven by the forces of what Marx would have called 'historical necessity' and it was the way we reacted that mattered – we must respect and reverence one another, and help one another to develop and be fulfilled – we had a long way to go but he felt that a great future lay ahead. Then Fred and Norman and one or two others began to speak about our great aim being 'technical efficiency' and all the other idealistic frills would come later. At that point I spoke – My best friend was killed in a raid over Hamburg on January 30th and to me that constituted a challenge. Can I answer that, by saying I'm aiming to become a technically efficient farmer? Surely, more is required than that. We must realise the responsibility our exemption imposes on us – how lucky we are even to be alive. The word 'service' has been derided, I said, but what higher aim can man have? I was rather worried that our farm meetings were being reduced to discussing when to kill Horace [the pig] and the amount of lard he would yield – spoken of with such relish, and I thought of my friend crashing to his death. Surely, I concluded, we have some higher purpose than to eat Horace in November.

In a pamphlet issued in 1948 explaining the work of the Frating Hall community, we are given a detailed description of the geology of the farm and the agricultural limitations and opportunities associated with it:

> Our soil is part of the alluvium and gravel beds of North-East Essex and South-East Suffolk, overlying brick earth and London clay. This strata is notoriously deficient in lime but is very responsive, and not easily damaged. As one walks from Clacton Road towards Frating church, our fields to the left and right are of poor sandy soils, over gravel, fields which can grow winter greens, early spuds, lucerne and so on. Really hungry land, requiring a constant supply of humus and chalk to make it hold moisture at all. Some twenty acres of this have rough woodland, scrub and gravel pit upon it.
>
> As one approaches the Hall and church, the soil steadily improves and deepens. Carrots, sugar beet, potatoes and corn can be grown well here, although we have three fields with a mixture of soils that give us a headache at crop-planning time: alluvium at one end, then sand, gravel, shale, brickearth and clay in a run of less than 100 yards! – a pipe drainer's nightmare.
>
> Generally, we find the soil requires constant ploughing or cultivating to keep it in fresh condition, because it has so little 'body' that it 'runs' and 'caps', after which moisture disappears and growth is inhibited. After four years of trying to rewrite the practice of agriculture in our own little perverse ways, we have come back to sound rotation, proper fallowing, the plough and the harrow.

There were twenty-one fields in all demarcated on the farm in the 1950s: Gravel Pit Field, Great Mill Field, Captain's Field, Alresford Bottoms, The Twenty Acres, Swingate & Long, Cottage Field, Church Field, Drive Field, Brakey Field,

Horse Meadow, Ram Field, Camp Field, Birch Field, Great Birchards Field, Middle Field, Rates Field, The Twenty-Seven Acre, and Frating Hall Wood. Each had its own distinctive shape and character.

Mistakes were made in the early days, as the community were the first to acknowledge. An 'ambitious and, consequently disastrous programme' in 1944 produced the decision to increase the herd of cows quickly, buying in two-year-old heifers, whose usefulness proved questionable and were sold at a loss. Turnover figures for 1943–1945 show how the community had to learn fast as to what activities were profitable and manageable, and which not. Sheep and pigs came and went without contributing anything to the farm's commercial viability. Poultry became profitable fairly early on, as did milk production from the small herd of Ayrshires they retained. Wheat and barley declined in quantities and sales, but potato sales increased in leaps and bounds. But it was egg production and salad greens that in some ways saved the farm from financial disaster in the first three years: thus the balance of cereals, livestock and market gardening began to change as fast as could be managed, given the timescale required in altering the crop rotation or the adaptation and cultivation of land for different uses.

Trevor Howard focused on poultry and egg production. When the core group arrived on the farm, they started with seventy hens; within a year they had 815, by 1948 there were 1,500 head of poultry. With poultry Howard was so successful that by the time he came to leave in 1952 the Frating Hall Farming Society won a national award for its expertise in breeding chickens for laying.

The mixed results from the first couple of years are reflected in a letter Joe Watson wrote to would-be member Kenneth Lambert on 2 May 1945:

Sorting potato crop at Frating Hall Farm, circa. 1947.

> We have had a troublesome Spring, chiefly due to illness. I have had a month off, first with a torn leg muscle, then kidney trouble. But we look like making a handsome profit. We have sold over £1000 of spuds and £500 greens up to date, and the harvest isn't in yet! This is without milk and eggs, another £1400. Of course, as you will realise, success brings its own problems. I am hoping that a bloke like you will do much to purge the egotism which is so rampant here, but I suppose we are not a bad crowd really. It's just that one reads of a tortured Europe and a selfish England, and one wants to heal the wounds a little, and help to remake England.

There were other trading activities too, notably a building team that not only constructed the accommodation required at Frating Hall for new members, but also did commercial work for neighbouring farms and others needing their services. A well-equipped woodworking shop developed a viable business, providing sheep hurdles, farm gates and other timber goods and services.

In a small printed report issued in 1946 called 'Three Years A-Growing', a note on the crop side of the business was positive:

> Crops have done well on the whole; sugar beet was well up on 1944; potatoes about the same and all corn returns showed improvement... Peas grown for picking did very well; for seed, quite well; runner beans for seed very badly. Lettuce was good, onions, or rather the failure thereof, made us cry; cauliflowers, spring and Xmas cabbage, good; and savoys, on which we are just starting, good.

As well as being a trading farm – a commercial enterprise – Frating Hall Farming Society was also trying to be a community, in which personal relationships were deemed as important as the jobs that people did. In addition, there was a degree of collective responsibility for the success of the whole endeavour – which in itself took time and effort – including pastoral care for each other as well as the children. There was a disproportionate number of children compared with the number of adults, unsurprising given the age of many of the early members, most of whom came as young married couples. On this issue there was a clear policy however: that childcare was not a collective responsibility. A short minute written by Marian Crosfield in 1951 recapitulated the basic principles of the Frating Hall community on the issue of childcare:

> Unlike most cooperative communities, no provision has been made for educating the children within the community. There is no Kindergarten, Kid Colony or Children's House. The children when they are old enough go to the village school. So far, the children have been young, mostly under five, and as yet I feel the community has not felt the full impact of its youngest members.

In the same year, things were still going well on the farming side, possibly even better than ever. In his 1951 Annual Report for the previous year to members, Joe Watson as Chairman of Directors records that:

> We have a very cheerful report to make for the year 1950. Our balance sheet shows a profit of £651. The heavy rainfall has been of great benefit to our light land. We are now a fully accredited Poultry Breeding Station, an achievement largely due to the patient efforts of our poultryman, Trevor Howard. Our herd of Ayrshire cows is now fully attested and their condition is a tribute to the work of Eric Tipper, the cowman. We grew a heavy crop of sugar beet, a record for the farm. One field of winter's oats grown on a Seed Contract gave a record yield for the district. A grand total of 175,935 eggs were produced during the year. Spring cabbage and cauliflower excelled among vegetables. A row of lime trees has been planted between the cottages and The Hall, and this, together with the new orchard, will add beauty to an already beautiful farm.

The avenue of lime trees still stands. Also recorded – unusual for a company report – is a record of marriages and children. There were now twelve married couples, fifteen children and 'the Staff at the Hall, ably presided over by Irene'. Irene Palmer was a stalwart of the Langham pioneers, a single woman, expert cook, expert tree-grafter, who stayed on until the end. Worthy of record too is the fact that 'only three of our members have been with us for less than five years, while seven of us have been here since the beginning'.

Janice Smith remembers Frating for the freedom she enjoyed there, between the age of four until the Watsons left when she was fifteen:

> It was an idyllic childhood actually because you had so much freedom, so much free space to do things. I remember telling the girls at the High School [Colchester County High School for Girls] how thrilled I was because they had called a calf after me, and they said: 'Do you mean you've got a cow named after you?' I thought that was fantastic. I could get the cows in, I could milk them. I didn't do it very often but I knew how to.

> Even so, at both the local primary school in Great Bentley and later secondary school, the Frating children were sometimes subject to ridicule or contempt because it was known that their parents refused to take part in the war directly. 'Father was a pacifist, as you know,' Janice told me, 'that's why people were so horrible to me at school.' On occasions the disagreements were closer to home. Peter Watson recalls sometimes being harassed by other children at Frating because of his father's prominent role on the farm, and the intensity of Joe Watson's beliefs.

Although Vera Brittain never lived there, her daughter did, no longer a child. In January 1948, eighteen-year-old Shirley Williams (then known as Shirley Catlin) went to Frating for six months as second cowman, in charge of 'a herd of Ayrshire dairy cows, handsome red-and-white animals of a certain temper'. Things did not go well at first. The head cowman was, she remembered, 'a pious Methodist who refused to work with a Catholic'. It was soon sorted out, possibly by Joe Watson, and the young Williams was impressed. 'I supposed I was a bit in love with Joe. I had never met anyone like him,' she recalled in her autobiography, *Climbing the Bookshelves*. Williams taught Janice how to ride a bike, and sent up to London for her own old bike which she gave to the young girl. Of Trevor Howard and his chickens, she wrote affectionately many years later 'he taught me that even hens have a personality'.

The children of Frating with two adults, 1947. From left to right: Richard Burrow, Mary 'Mip' Burrow, Paul Burrow, Janice Watson, Andrew Lambert, Hugh Lambert, Unknown, Phoebe Lambert, Anthony Wickenden, Katherine Howard, Christopher Wickenden.

This sympathetic relationship between community members and the animals, as evident in the naming of a calf after the young Janice, seemed part of the ethos of the farm. Apart from seeing the hens as individuals, as Williams witnessed, Howard named one of the cows Natasha, according to his daughter Katherine. 'Natasha was the person he loved most in all literature, he said, and so one of the cows was called Natasha.' This is from a letter Trevor Howard wrote to Enid on 1 November 1942 (All Saints Day):

> The cows are all well. This is the position. We have 3 new ones and Jenny, Blossom, and Dido have gone to Langham (as have the calves and 10 of my best pullets). We got them off one morning but, the

> same night I had a frantic phone call – 'come over at once the cows are all over place and won't give their milk'. So, I rushed over in the car extracted what milk I could and went back the next morning and milked them out and they are now doing O.K. You should see Joe with them. He's as pleased as punch, driving them up the road as much as to say, 'just look at my cows'. As for the replacements there is 'Stella' the 'black and white beastie' milking very well. Very large, the others play games of 'Tig' running under her tummy. Then there's Maria, a fleshy vulgar Victorian barmaid sort of cow! a nearly all black (hence the subtle name) shorthorn X. a fairish milker. Then lastly there's 'Janet' a sweet little deer-like Jersey heifer with the prettiest face and markings you ever saw! But at the business end, little milk!

This personalisation has a long history, and is not just sentimentality or childish anthropomorphism, but part of a tradition of seeing domesticated animals as human familiars or part of God's providence. The historian Keith Thomas recorded this kindly sentiment in his wonderful study *Man and the Natural World*, drawing examples from Essex, where on small farms all stock animals had proper names, though not human ones: 'In Tudor Essex there were cattle called Gentle, Brown Snout, Old White Lock, Button and Lovely.' On the other hand, there was a harsh reality about the ultimate fate of animals. Peter Watson remembers 'a pig hanging upside down in the barn slit down the middle with the blood being caught in a wheelbarrow'.

Phoebe Lambert, like Janice Smith, was another member who remembered her childhood at Frating as a time of enormous personal freedom.

> I was born in 1942 and my family joined the community in early 1945 before the war ended. My father wanted to join a community to work on the land which he had been doing with my

mother. They already had 2 children, me and my brother Hugh, who was then only two years old, and so my father was searching around to engage in some sort of farming work. He had already failed two [conscription] tribunals. He failed because the Tribunal panel felt that his ideological reasons against the taking of human life were not strong enough to grant him exception. He therefore had a lot of difficulty resisting conscription until he could find a 'reserved occupation'.

It was an extraordinary way to grow up, and as children we were totally free. I know I used to get up at 5 or 6 in the morning and go down into the woods or the spinney, and scoop up tadpoles in the streams, or watercress, or gather mushrooms to bring back for breakfast.

Frating was really like an extended family and there were always going to be tensions. And of course there were some very strong personalities amongst people who were prepared to go to prison for their beliefs and to suffer as pariahs outside. Frating was a tiny place. My mother was interviewed about the war years in the 70s and she said she'd never been more isolated in her life. It was hard being considered beyond the pale and to suffer taunts and whisperings such as: 'Oh, it's those communists down the road,' and 'those conchies', that sort of thing.

I think as children we were protected from the outside world by our families but nevertheless in those early years there was amongst all the community members and their visitor friends huge optimism, huge conviviality and a great sense that anything was possible.

Other farmers in the nearby vicinity kept their distance. For instance, the kids on the farm used to go scrumping in the orchards of some of the surrounding farms and there would be hell to pay because we had gone onto their territory. There was a sense that we existed in a kind of capsule.

Similarly, Katherine Weaver remembered an extraordinary sense of freedom growing up: 'We were outdoors all the time, either playing or even working. As a child I helped out on the farm when needed, potato-picking, collecting eggs, watering and feeding the chickens.' She said that, perhaps unusually, she can remember the great barn more than the cottage the family lived in, because she spent so much time with the other children in and around the barn. She also recollected that time spent indoors was often spent in other children's houses, where they would pop in for tea, as and when they felt like it. 'It was like having more parents,' she remembered, a confirmation of the truism that it takes a village to raise a child. The children had their own habitat, their own social world, and their own moral domain. There were trips to the seaside by lorry or van. On one occasion the children were taken to Frinton, then known for its snobbery towards visitors. At the railway crossing which marks the resort's main entrance road, Katherine recalled, whoever was driving the vehicle rolled the window down and remarked to someone standing at the roadside: 'Lovely day, isn't it?' 'I don't believe we have been introduced,' was the cold reply.

There were accidents of course. Phoebe Lambert remembers that she and Katherine Howard 'were playing in the fields at haymaking time and one of the boys was playing with a pitch fork, a frightening looking object with a long handle and two steel prongs at one end of it. It was designed to pick up hay which would then be pitched onto small stacks. But that day the pitch fork caught Kathy in her throat – in fact it had pierced her jugular vein and blood spurted like a fountain from the hole it had made.' In panic Phoebe ran to the next field calling for help, where Katherine's father Trevor was working. He came running, 'faster than I had ever seen him run, scooped her up in his arms and with his free hand he placed his thumb over the hole in her neck. She would have died but for her father's prompt action.'

Sadly, there was one incident in the late 1940s, this time fatal, which cast a shadow over the community for a long time. On an outing to Brightlingsea, the youngest of four children belonging to the Burrow family drowned in a boating accident. Phoebe Lambert recalls the incident and its impact clearly. 'I remember the effect it had on everybody. And the funeral for the little boy – we as children were not allowed to go which is a shame. I do remember the funeral procession coming across the fields to the church, as it was like the processions we had every year at harvest time.'

Apart from the children's sense of freedom, members of the community probably ate better than most others during the long years of wartime food-rationing, another helpful by-product of farm work. Janice Smith recalls:

> When we were living in the Hall, where all the single people lived, we always had a cooked breakfast. Farm work was quite hard and farm workers got greater rations than most other people. The diet was pretty good for someone in wartime. We didn't have powdered eggs, we had real eggs. And every household could have half a pig, so you would make that last for ever. A bacon and egg breakfast was very common because you were having to do very heavy work. Farm workers were allowed much bigger cheese rations.
>
> All the produce in the kitchen garden – an absolutely stunning walled kitchen garden next to the Hall – well all the fruit and vegetables grown there were distributed for free to those on the farm. There was a big walnut tree outside the house and there would be a ritual shaking of the tree and the distribution of the nuts; likewise with the cherry tree. All this was distributed for nothing. People paid for their milk, or chicken, but vegetables were free. And of course most of the houses on the farm had a garden as well.

The walnut tree was still standing forty years later, but in the 1980s became diseased and had to be cut down. The cherry trees also went at some point but have been replaced, which would have made Chekhov happy.

Laborare est orare: work is prayer

The community was keen to review the farming project as a work in progress, and in minutes, letters and the occasional pamphlet printed for supporters and others, the story of the Frating Hall community unfolded before the public eye. In a letter written by Joe Watson in December 1945, and circulated as a formal Christmas message of achievement, the Christian ethos is strong, almost overpoweringly so. But everything Joe wrote, whether privately or publicly, is knitted together by a self-critical redemptive morality.

This Christmas letter includes a shot across the bows of the blood-and-soil movement which had been gaining ground in rural England in the 1930s, disturbingly so. Eventually the association with pro-German sentiment, antisemitism and direct links with extreme nationalist organisations caused the movement to be quashed by the government at the outbreak of the Second World War. 'Our refusal to ally ourselves to the romanticism of compostoloy, organicitis, and squirarchitus, and run tractors, use fertilisers, and milk by machinery,' Joe wrote, 'did not mean that we were blind to what Berdyaev calls "Telluric mysticism", oneness with the earth and the living organism of Nature.' On these matters, pragmatism was the order of the day.

In 1946 the community printed its 'Three Years A-Growing' review. Joe once again wrote the main article and recorded with genuine pleasure that 'It would be false of me to pretend that a stocktaking after three years at Frating is other than a delight.' Particularly welcome was the claim that 'the difficulty of becoming part of village life has been overcome'.

The success with poultry and egg production, and with market gardening, had, it seemed, turned local scepticism to grudging acceptance if not admiration. Joe, as always, adopted a Lawrentian turn of phrase, when he wrote in despair that 'The world has become a vast drug store, with initials to kill every germ, and medicines to cure all ills, but nowhere in the entire pharmacy is there one little grain of life.' For Watson, Berdyaev nevertheless remained his principal touchstone, invariably providing the text for his communal sermons, and he concluded with hopes for the future by citing the Russian Christian anarchist yet again: 'Only love turns a man towards the future, frees him from the shackles of the past, and is a means of creating a new and better life.'

Joe's wife Doris was at this time equally optimistic. 'Spring and Summer passed in a whirl of work and sunshine. Visitors came to help with the harvest and to keep us from losing touch with our fellow-men. As the days shortened, sing-songs around the common-room fire led to the forming of our choir, which bids fair to becoming famous locally.' And that was true. Choral singing and communal singing were enormously popular during the war, and the Frating Hall choir not only enlivened and gladdened church services at Frating and in churches elsewhere in the neighbourhood, but were soon after joined by the Frating Hall Players who produced and mounted plays in the great barn open to all. This also helped heal the breach with neighbours and villagers nearby, if not England entire.

6. High days and holy days

> The East Anglian wind does far more than move the barley; it is doctrinal.
>
> RONALD BLYTHE, *Akenfield*, 1969

Wash the sea, wash the sky

Life at Frating was leavened by harvest festivals, choral concerts, christenings, productions of Shakespeare and the annual arrival of a new cohort of idealistic volunteers helping with the harvest. If life sometimes seemed only jolly for the children, there were cakes and ale for the adults too, and there was always something going on, particularly in the summer when visitors arrived, and a lively and flamboyant group of visitors they appear to have been. In addition to the gaiety that accompanied them, like everybody else they too had to work their passage. According to Phoebe Lambert:

> From the start the church was pivotal both as a place of worship but also as an arts centre for the very creative community and their fellow pacifists, several of whom had international reputations as artists and musicians. The highlights of the year were the dramatic events and festivals and parties performed in the barn as well as the concerts in the common room, in the Hall and in the church.

Taking their cue from the success of The Adelphi Players at Langham, which had gained a name for touring Shakespeare round the villages mentioned earlier, Frating quickly established its own choir and dramatic society,

The Frating Players, to which Lambert's parents belonged. It is hard to overestimate the importance amateur theatre played in British life in the first half of the twentieth century, especially so within political and religious circles: whether as plays, pageants or masques. In the early days of local theatre, many were being formed to put on plays felt to contain a social message, particularly in the North East of England. The Stockport Garrick Society set up its own Little Theatre in 1901 and claimed to be the first amateur group to perform the plays of Ibsen and Shaw. The People's Theatre in Newcastle upon Tyne set up the Clarion Dramatic Society in 1911 to raise money for the British Socialist Society, producing plays by Shaw, Galsworthy, Ibsen and Synge. In Liverpool and London, left-wing Unity Theatres were established as full-blown repertory theatres. Across Britain towns and cities started their own 'Little Theatres'.

Equally active was the Village Drama Society which by 1939 claimed some 600 local companies. It was started by Mary Kelly (on whom Virginia Woolf modelled her character Miss La Trobe in her 1941 novel about village pageants, *Between the Acts*), Kelly was unstinting in her enthusiasm for amateur theatre, publishing *How to Make a Pageant* in 1936 and *Village Theatre* in 1939. A recent essay by historian Andrew Walker on Kelly's central role in encouraging amateur theatre in the first half of the twentieth century highlighted the relationship between rural drama and rural religious life and traditions.

Like T.S. Eliot and many of those associated with the Religious Drama Society, formed in 1928, Kelly believed that religious communities provided the lifeblood of rural dramatic works, grounded, as they are, in the rhythms of both the ecumenical calendar and the natural progression of the seasons.

Production of Twelfth Night in the barn. From left to right: Derek Crosfield, Enid Howard, Irene Palmer, Trevor Howard, person unknown.

The Frating community came from backgrounds which – though few had experience of higher education – were nevertheless highly literate and familiar with the performative drama of church, stage and choral concert. Most had been schooled in a culture of literary and political magazines and pamphlets, and knew their liturgy, catechisms and hymnals. They could discuss, debate, occasionally act, and all could sing. I have been unable to discover exactly which plays – apart from those of Shakespeare – were performed and toured, though The Adelphi Players had certainly put on productions of J.M. Synge's *Deirdre of the Sorrows* and *The Unknown Warrior*, and indeed Joe Watson mentions enjoying these two performances in his Christmas letter of December 1945. In the 'Frating Hall Community' newsletter one contributor writes that 'Our dramatic activities started with play-readings.' At the Harvest Festival in 1945 a small group of members staged a scene from *King Lear*. This was followed by a full-length production of *Twelfth Night*, and then came *The Taming of the Shrew*, *Henry IV, Part I* and T.S. Eliot's *Murder in The Cathedral*, which Phoebe Lambert.

Both Phoebe Lambert's parents were members of The Frating Players, and she remembers them 'going over and over their lines as they went round the fields collecting eggs and shutting up the hens'. She particularly recalls a production of *As You Like It*: 'My mother played Rosalind, and in another Shakespeare play, *Henry IV, Part I*, my father played Falstaff, and in another Sir Toby Belch with a cushion stuffed up his shirt.' Other members of the farm played different parts. These productions took place in the barn and the audience sat on bales of straw which provided the seating for everybody. On one occasion there were rats running across the stage and my father was batting them off and saying to the audience, 'It's only a few hundred rats.' Some sixty years after, Phoebe Lambert still speaks of 'some extraordinary performances – T.S. Eliot's *Murder in the Cathedral*, for example – they performed this in the church. I was very, very young but I remember a battering ram being literally heaved against the church doors! It was quite frightening. My mother was part of the chorus and she was singing, "Wash the sea, wash the sky!"'

Janice Watson remembered the rats, and how they were disposed of: 'Every so often they had to clear the barn of them – of which there were hundreds.' To accomplish this a hose was run from the tractor's exhaust into the barn, and the farm workers and others waited for the rats to come running out to be killed. Piles of dead rats were put into pits and their bodies incinerated. Such mass infestations were not uncommon. In his memoir *A Good Living*, Hugh Barrett recalls a similar episode at another farm where he worked. Having come across a dozen or more rats in the milking shed in the small hours, and with one other worker having killed 'scores' within the first half hour, they had to call for extra help:

> For the rest of the day six men, a horde of kids and heaven knows how many dogs killed and killed, first round the buildings, barn, yards and pens and then up in the paddocks. How many? Hundreds for sure, perhaps a thousand. (They were gathered in heaps but no one was keen to count them.)

The plays in the great barn were also remembered by Janice: 'At Frating they did a Shakespeare play once a year and a modern play, and perhaps one by Somerset Maugham. They did it in the big barn. The curtains were made of dyed hessian sacks, the ones used for storing potatoes.' Gaining confidence, the Frating Players ventured further afield, giving performances at Nayland Sanatorium, Great Bentley, and at a school in Colchester.

The tradition, which began at Langham continued elsewhere, in addition to Frating. Murry took his theatrical skills to his next project, the communal farm at Theltenham, where a new cohort of eager farmers started their own theatre troupe. 'We produced another play,' Murry wrote in *Community Farm*, 'and boldly took it to two of the neighbouring villages: whereby we made a profit of £30 for the village hall fund, which in its two years of existence has managed to accumulate over £400. Now we are in rehearsal again, for the farmhouse players, in which I am the low comedian, have become an institution.' As we know, the actor Jim Broadbent had grown up in a pacifist settlement in Lincolnshire at approximately the same time, one that also had its own strong theatrical traditions. Like some of the Frating children, Broadbent had also been educated at Leighton Park School, the Quaker school in Reading. It is interesting to see how much of Broadbent's subsequent stage and screen work has been with directors such as Mike Leigh and Ken Loach, where strong ensemble playing around important social themes has been a key factor.

Reading and storytelling

In the early 1960s, Trevor and Enid's daughter Katherine began to ask her parents about their memories of Frating, as it seemed to have played such an important part in their lives:

> While I was still at school I became very interested in the background to Frating, to try and make sense of who my father was, so I asked him various questions and he gave me a list of books which led me to D.H. Lawrence and Tolstoy. He did it in a very subtle way. He gave me the letters of D.H. Lawrence when I was ill on holiday once – I was only about 12 or 13 – and this was a way of saying you can write letters in a different way. So I read an awful lot of Lawrence.

From Katherine's memories it became clear that apart from farm work, Trevor Howard continued to indulge his love of reading. 'I was very aware of my father's love of Tolstoy's work and I've inherited some of his books about, and by, Tolstoy,' Katherine continued. In letters from her father to her mother before marriage, now in her possession, she recalls that he wrote about Tolstoy's philosophy to his future wife Enid. 'He mostly writes about *War and Peace*,' she said, 'which they were both listening to (in different places a long way from each other) in a serialised version on the radio.' Even when busy on the farm Howard was:

> Lecturing and leading WEA [Workers' Educational Association] literature courses. He suggested to my mother that they should put together a series of lectures on 'Blake, Whitman, Tolstoy, Lawrence – Prophets of a New World' into which they would introduce their own 'philosophy of Life, spiritually speaking'.

However, Katherine qualified this by adding:

> 'But actually he was most convincing talking about the pleasures of real physical work – on the land.'

In addition to a continuing study of Christian literature and philosophy, Joe Watson remained keen to spread the word by encouraging others to read what he regarded as the most compelling books of the time. In 'A Good Workman and his Friends: Recollections of John Middleton Murry', the former steelworker wrote that 'D.H. Lawrence has meant more to me than any other man, except Jesus.' But there were other writers in his canon. In his Christmas Letter of December 1945, Watson adds 'a personal note':

> I am indebted more than I can say to the following books: *Slavery and Freedom* by Berdyaev; *The Woman Who Was Poor* by Leon Bloy; *Shelley*, by our own Frank Lea and a novel, *The Horse's Mouth*, by Joyce Cary.

On another occasion Watson recalled that 'I was reared in poverty, but had Jesus, Blake, Lawrence and Berdyaev, in that order, to sustain me.' It seems astonishing that Watson – in addition to his work as farm manager – not only found time to keep up with his reading, work with the choir, travel the local churches as a lay preacher, and be active in the Labour Party, but also found time to correspond with a wide range of writers and thinkers, nationally and internationally. One of them, according to son Peter, was the renowned Austrian Jewish philosopher of existentialism, Martin Buber.

It is hard to imagine that this was a time when people literally changed their lives as a result of reading novels – and there was one novelist whose work was read with the same intensity as many might read the scriptures. That novelist was D.H. Lawrence. Middleton Murry, undoubtedly Lawrence's most devoted disciple despite all the fallings out, wrote persuasively that Lawrence's work could only be understood as a whole:

> For their unity lies in the fact that they are a spiritual autobiography of a man of extraordinary genius who has committed the whole of himself to the search for a new mode of human existence, a new consciousness, a new religion.

Max Plowman was of the same mind. In 'The Significance of D.H. Lawrence', an essay published in *The Adelphi* in June 1930, he wrote of the impact Lawrence's writings made when they were first published in Georgian England, following the political and military catastrophes of the First World War. Plowman, a veteran of the Somme, saw the light when one day, in his own words, he 'walked out of the army' in 1917, and, in a phrase used by Middleton Murry, 'stepped clean out of the mechanical and inhuman shambles into which war had been prostituted'. For Plowman, and many of the novelist's most ardent followers, Lawrence was a god come to alert the world to a new era of mechanisation of body and spirit:

> Right in the centre of the vortex of mechanisation stood D.H. Lawrence, protesting against this blasphemy against life and proclaiming the Holy Ghost in man as the only source of instinctive purity… Taking up his position at the centre of the vortex, he stood at the point where it finds its ultimate challenge; and it is from this point that the contrary movement, outward, in widening circles of creative life, will begin.

And it did begin. Following the end of the war, the Lawrentian 'moment' seemed to have arrived, aided by the growing interest in Freud's theories, in increasing public sexual frankness, while eventually gaining serious purchase in intellectual life via the academy. Lawrence's radical world-view first entered the universities through the work of the literary critics F.R. and Queenie Leavis and the many others belonging to the arts and education establishment, especially in the field of extra-mural or continuing education aimed at working-class students. Lawrence stood for life, for nature, for sexual freedom, for breaking the chains of class oppression and allowing people to live freely for the first time. There had been no other writer like him.

Both Watson and Howard, despite coming from very different backgrounds likewise took Lawrence as such a prophet. As we saw, Katherine Weaver's father encouraged her to read Lawrence from an early age, particularly the letters and poems, though she read the novels too. Given that her father was an only child from a respectable Church of England family who went to a series of boarding schools with religious and even military connections, it is astonishing that the work of D.H. Lawrence proved so important in shaping his understanding of the world and the wish to change it. But Lawrence had that effect on many in the first half of the twentieth century, and it is difficult to think of any other novelist before or after who exercised this extraordinary existential power. Here is a letter John Macmurray wrote to a friend, John Roberts, on 10 October 1930:

> I've been profoundly moved by the work of D.H. Lawrence. Have you tried to estimate it seriously? It is having a great influence on masses of young people here, and I expect also in America.

Macmurray's enthusiasm for Lawrence is further confirmed when on 13 June 1933, shortly after attending a dinner following a lecture the Scottish philosopher had given, Plowman wrote to Middleton Murry that 'He [Macmurray] confessed to us last night that D.H. Lawrence had meant more to him than anybody.' These were almost identical to the words Joe Watson had used. And if reading Lawrence produced this effect, imagine what it was like to have known him in person. Frank Lea's essay on Lawrence in his 1975 collection *Voices in the Wilderness: From Poetry to Prophecy in Britain*, gathers together the memories of those who knew Lawrence personally, and for whom,

> Being in Lawrence's company they say, was like breathing a rarer atmosphere, in which the most everyday activities took on a new animation, the most commonplace objects a radiance. Not only did he see things as though for the first time, but he empowered others to do so.

As important was Lea's assertion that Lawrence's work was gaining a serious readership beyond conventional literary circles:

> In the 1920s and 30s, the working man was his eagerest [sic] reader: it was not until the 1950s that the dons caught on to him and pinned him out for dissection. Before and during the last war, I used to meet north-country miners who saved up to buy his books as they came out, and whose families no doubt, still possess most of the first editions. And those men read him, not only for his marvellous evocations of the life they knew best, but for his conclusions as a writer and a man.

Lea does not offer an opinion as to whether the miners' wives also read Lawrence, which they may well have done. The expansion of the branch library network in Britain in the 1930s was to meet the demands of a new reading public, in which women readers played the largest part. Novels such as *Sons and Lovers*, *The Rainbow*, *Women in Love* – controversial, sexually frank and much discussed – would have been keenly sought after.

Younger children also participated in the interest in books and reading. 'What I most remember about the visitors we had was whether they were good storytellers,' Janice Watson told me. 'One family – the father was the music librarian at the BBC, so he could get multiple copies of choral works for Dad's choir – well, they had a son who was disabled, and they used to come all summer long, though the father stayed in London for work during the week. I remember the mother used to read all the Arthur Ransome books to her son, Howard, and I was allowed to join them and listen.' Janice's brother Peter particularly remembers Sid Chaplin's frequent visits to Frating with his family. 'Sid was a great raconteur, and I loved listening to him and my father swapping stories of people and situations they had known. Sid claimed his storytelling ability stemmed from having to tell bed-time stories to his siblings when he was young. He was one of my favourite bed-time story readers, as he made the tales come alive.'

Other friends and visitors

Composer William 'Billy' Wordsworth – a distant descendant of the Lakeland poet of the same name – was another regular visitor to the farm. After the war Wordsworth had settled in Hindhead, and it was there that Joe and his family would often travel and so 'made friends with musicians like Dennis Brain, Julian Bream and Desmond Dupré', according to Peter Watson. These were amongst the leading virtuoso musicians of their time, and the young Watson remembered that 'Many of these people came to the farm and I was privileged to hear them play.' For such visitors, especially during wartime, Frating must have seemed a sanctuary, or haven of peace and security. Highly regarded as a composer of symphonies and large orchestral pieces still being performed and recorded today, Wordsworth wrote a dedicated 'Valediction' in commemoration of Joe Watson following Watson's death in 1966, and played at Watson's funeral.

Open-air concert practice in the Hall garden.

The musical life at Frating was impressive, not unconnected with the political and religious affiliations of many artists and musicians at the time, affiliations which often included a commitment to pacifism, the most famous being Benjamin Britten. In addition to Brain, Bream and Dupré, other stellar names who attached themselves to the Frating community included Charles Craig, Alexander Gibson and Imogen Holst. Craig (1919–1997) came from an unusual background for the world of classical opera. The youngest of fifteen children born in Hackney, he famously said he'd practised singing on Hackney Marshes. He was not a pacifist but on joining up was recruited to ENSA. Afterwards, he became the lead tenor at Covent Garden, later making many recordings and performing at opera houses throughout the world, standing in for Placido Domingo on several occasions. Janice Watson said that Craig came to regard her parents as his own, visiting Frating as often as he could. Also close to the Watsons was Alexander Gibson, another celebrated musician with a prestigious career that culminated in becoming the longest-serving Principal Conductor of the Royal Scottish Symphony Orchestra, honoured with a knighthood, and a legendary figure in Glasgow's musical life. He visited Frating whenever possible and joined in the musical life there, as did Imogen Holst, who arranged and conducted choral recitals at the farm.

One of the prisoners-of-war, John Vostatek, settled happily at Frating. A Sudeten ethnic German living in Czechoslovakia, he was conscripted into the German army and was captured early on in the war. An engineer by training, he worked hard at the farm and contributed to the life of the community, despite being a rather private man. After the war he found a job as an engineer in Colchester and remained in contact with some of his former friends until the end of his life. He was very artistic, Phoebe Lambert remembered; Paul Burrow is in possession of a fine painting by Vostatek of the Great Barn, one of a number he painted whilst at Frating. He taught Phoebe Lambert's parents how to weave, eventually helping them construct a loom on which they became skilled enough to sell woven goods to Heals and Liberty in London.

One regular visitor, Mary Duncan, kindly set down in writing her memories of her visits to Frating between 1943 and 1947:

> For four or five summers – I cannot exactly remember the dates – during the war and its immediate aftermath, I went to Frating to help with the harvest. It was a wonderful change from taking a local job at the Ministry of Pensions, which, with the new recruits to the RAF, and the predictable crowd of holiday makers, overran Blackpool in the summer.
>
> I suppose the first thing to be said about Frating was the sense of freedom. It was everything that Blackpool was not – empty, peaceful, pretty. I loved the old farmhouse which in my memory was not very

near to any other habitations, and conveyed a sense of space everywhere. The days were full of variety – and variety, in that context, is an aspect of freedom. The main job was to bring in the harvest, building the sheaves into stooks as they were thrown out of the binder – all this done by hand, of course, in those days. Then, after some days, tossing the sheaves with a pitchfork onto horse-drawn carts. The swing of the pitch fork, from ground to cart, was very satisfying: especially with oats. Wheat was heavy and barley though light, was spikey. Briefly I remember doing a spell of milking (by hand); and joy of joys, riding a slow horse to the blacksmiths to be shod – the horse, that is. In all this there was a lot of tomfoolery, and a sense of working on the harvest field together. I do not remember any serious quarrelling. There were arguments and disagreements – about work, say; or, at table, about belief systems, convictions, or other people. Folk could be trying, even critical, but always interesting. United in their attitude to war, they were free to be themselves in community.

We used to get lots of visitors at the weekends, mostly from London. I remember clearing out a byre with Shirley Williams – not quite Williams then, and I remember thinking how pretty she was. My most bewitching memory of the impact of the visitors was on a glorious morning when most people, Saturday though it was, were already at work. I heard the sound of a violin and following it, came to the large drawing room which, having windows on two sides, was filled with sunshine. The place was deserted except for a figure in the centre of the room. It was Jürgen Hess, who later became the leader of the BBC Scottish Orchestra, playing Beethoven – the Violin Concerto. It was such a beautiful moment. I also remember two sisters, singers who were regular visitors, I remember the song that one of them sang, though I have never heard it sung again.

The sun on my right hand
And the moon on the other –
The moon is my Sister
The sun is my Brother.

The sun on my left hand
And the moon on my right –
My Brother, good morning
My Sister, good night.

There were spats and fall-outs among us but in our leisure hours harmony prevailed. We used to sit together in the drawing room if nothing else was going on, reading our books – George Orwell, Herbert Read, Reinhold Niebuhr, or something a bit lighter. This is rather a rosy account and, as I was only around in the summer, an incomplete one. But I remember a sense of family, the connectedness of people which was a fundamental aspect of the community – people who were thoughtful, responsible, caring, often merry. But all of them as I recall, were serious people, people of conviction and humanity.

Liturgy and ritual

Most but not all of those who arrived at Frating professed Christian beliefs, though with varying doctrinal affiliations. Joe Watson was, perhaps surprisingly, firmly Church of England, though his wife Doris came from a strong Methodist background, and was not always comfortable with Anglican ceremony. 'They stand up too much,' she used to say somewhat drily, according to daughter Janice. We know that Shirley Williams, arriving for a six-month stay, had to overcome the initial coldness of the head cowman, a pious nonconformist deeply suspicious of her Catholicism. Given that visitors and short-term residents included Jewish refugees, Frating was required to be ecumenical. This may be why gatherings for prayers and reflection were more often held in the secular space of the great barn rather than in Frating church itself, even though it was no more than 200 yards away.

Once settled, a friend of those at Frating recalls: 'It was decided to improvise the old historic barn for use as a church with an altar table and harvest decorations beautifully arranged. Then it was decided to begin the Harvest Festival with a brief religious ceremony in which Frating children made offerings to the altar.' That person, an early supporter who became the community's dedicated minister, was the Reverend Hugh A. Davison. He recalled his early enthusiasm for the project:

> The impression left with me was that the Community could not survive without a more reverent acceptance of the Christian tradition and attachment to some established Church. It was a surprise to be asked to take the Harvest Festival the following year at Frating. I don't remember very much about this visit, save that the Harvest Home supper loomed much more important than the worship. I still had serious doubts about worship striking any real roots in the life of the Community. However I came away with a deep interest and liking for the folks I had met and a resolve to pray for the place – which I have kept ever since.

Trevor Howard recorded that:

> Our Harvest Festivals have been perhaps the most outstanding, especially when the Rev Hugh Davison has been down to conduct the thanksgiving service and inspire other activities. In the last two years proceedings have taken place in the barn. Last year, we built a large open fireplace, so that the huge centuries-old barn presented a glowing picture: a roaring log fire, the barn decorated with sheaves of corn and berries, tables laid with Irene's culinary masterpieces, surrounded by over eighty guests, made up the scene I shall always remember. Supper was followed by songs and games, and a scene acted from *King Lear*.

Choir practice in the barn, conducted by Joe Watson, circa. 1950.

Phoebe Lambert's parents Joanna and Kenneth were not religious, but early on became close friends with Hugh Davison, who often stayed at their house when he visited the farm, or later on when they had left, to their next home in Colchester. She told me that:

> Although my parents were secular pacifists and therefore had not christened us three children as babies, they decided in 1948, probably with Hugh Davison's influence, that we as children should be baptised so that we had the option of being brought up as C of E which we could accept or reject in later life. On this basis Hugh Davison agreed to christen us and in the great barn he performed the ceremony. As a six- and five-year-old, I and my brother Hugh stood on the earth-damp barn floor. I remember us looking up to the rafters of the barn and at this immensely tall man in his impressive vestments ready to baptise

> us with holy water from a makeshift font but Andrew Max (named after Max Plowman), still not yet two, had to stand on a chair to receive his baptism.

But some Frating members were keen to worship at the adjacent church when possible, though the regular congregation was extremely small, due in part to the fact that the church was some distance from the village and few villagers had cars in those days, and had to walk. In bad weather many chose otherwise. 'We shared the clergy for Frating Church with Thorrington,' Janice Smith said, 'which is the next village.' She went on to describe the slightly haphazard arrangements for taking the service:

> My father was churchwarden for the lack of anybody else doing it. He remembers going there one day for the eight o'clock Sunday morning service, and there were the vicar's footprints in the snow going up and going back to the church door. He'd gone. Nobody had turned up and he'd gone home.
>
> The vicar was a very charismatic preacher but he only had three sermons, so we got to learn them all off by heart. He often started by staring into a corner, saying 'I can see Him there, my friend,' referring to Jesus. People who hadn't seen him before thought he was marvellous and we were lucky to have him, but he wasn't much cop as a vicar.

Coincidentally Hugh Barrett recalls the vicar in another village church, this time in Suffolk, who similarly spoke familiarly of 'having breakfast alone in the church with Jesus every morning', or how 'he'd seen Him more than once under the trees in the churchyard'. The unearthly and the quotidian seemed to flourish in many of these smaller, isolated rural hamlets and villages where life was still more elemental than we might think. It helps to remember that as late as 1942, one in three English villages still lacked piped water, though Frating was better served than that in most services, if not all.

Like Trevor Howard, Watson became keen to become more formally recognised as an Anglican officiate, though unlike Howard he did not seek training and ordination in order to become a full-time priest. To this end, according to daughter Janice, a meeting was arranged with the local bishop who had sought Joe out:

> I don't know how my father managed to see the Bishop of Colchester, but the Bishop said, 'Right, Joe, I need you to be a lay reader,' and my father said, 'Well I haven't done any exams since I was twelve.' Anyway he did the exams and passed two, and they said, 'That's alright, you can still be one.' He used to go around various places in the Manningtree area as an itinerant preacher, and the people used to send these letters to J.H. Watson, Esq., M.A., and he used to say he wasn't an M.A., and they said 'well you are one to us.'

It is the cultural life of the Frating community that in retrospect redeems many of the difficulties of the farming practicalities and personal differences for those who lived there. In his 1962 letter to his daughter Katherine, already cited, Trevor Howard repeats how much he treasured this aspect of the family's time at Frating:

> It was about all in the singing and those roped in from outside and to a much lesser extent in the plays, that the community really shone and of course all its forces were gathered together for the great Harvest Festivals in the barn with its wonderful decorations. Hugh Davison preaching like a prophet sent from God, and a galaxy of stars in the very threshold of stardom as singers, instrumentalists and conductors – the suppers, the services, the post supper activities. I don't think we will ever see days like those again and I thank God for the privilege of having been part of them.

Harvest supper in the barn.

The long hours and hard work on the farm, together with a hectic programme of meetings, services and festive occasions, may have led the community to becoming somewhat inward-looking or defensive, despite overcoming the suspicions of their neighbours. For almost at the same time as Frating got into its stride, the Othona Community was established in 1946 at Bradwell on the Blackwater estuary, less than twenty miles away. It appears no contact was ever made between the two. Established by the charismatic former RAF padre Norman Motley to bring together British and German Christians in a spirit of reconciliation, Othona established an 'open Christian community' which still thrives today, welcoming people to a 'place with a pattern of work, worship, study and play where people of different beliefs, cultures, classes, abilities and ages can discover how to live together'. Starting life in a small collection of abandoned army huts, today it is self-sufficient enough to operate successfully off-grid, and environmental sustainability has been fully joined with its therapeutic ambitions as a spiritual retreat. The two settlements would surely have had much in common to discuss and share, but sadly this never happened.

Despite the insularity experienced by some members at times, Frating was a rich and stimulating environment for its children. This may well have caused envy amongst some of their schoolfriends at the village primary school, and later at high school; on the other hand, it may have reinforced the idea that the children of Frating were living amongst some very strange and possibly suspect people. All Frating children attended the local primary school in Great Bentley, and several went to one of the Colchester grammar schools or to Quaker schools at Saffron Walden or Reading. Others went elsewhere, taking with them experiences of life and a diversity of adult friends and familiars that few of their generation could match. In their many and varied ways, the children who grew up at Frating went on to pursue lives of vocation, whether in the field of artistic, educational or humanitarian causes and endeavours.

Potato sorting.

7. New lives, new landscapes

> Life is an experimental journey, undertaken involuntarily. It's a journey of the mind through matter, and since it is the mind that journeys, it's there one lives. Thus there are contemplative souls that have lived more intensely, more extensively and more turbulently than souls that live externally. The end result is what counts. What was felt is what was lived.
>
> FERNANDO PESSOA, *The Book of Disquiet*, 1982

Coming to the end

The memories of the Frating group were emotions recollected in tranquillity; all those I spoke to had been children during its formative years. Yet reading family correspondence, together with the minutes of the cooperative's meetings, annual reports and occasional newsletters, it seems to have been for many of the adults a life of hard work, occasional bad luck and periods of internal strife – but also times of great, even transcendental, joy. To add to their worries, as pacifists and 'conchies', Frating members were regarded as 'pariahs' by others nearby – the word used by Phoebe Lambert – though over time this changed as the community won the respect of its farming neighbours. Since we will never know with certainty how the adults contemplated upon their great experiment in later years – though Joe Watson and Trevor Howard did sometimes reflect on it publicly, the former with a mixture of achievement and frustration, the latter with regretful affection – the children who became the adults I interviewed remain gripped and fascinated by the experience. None expressed reservations about my wish to revisit this story, and were as excited by the idea as I was. They were, without exception, proud of what their parents had achieved, even at the cost of the anxieties it caused. As we have already seen, even as a schoolgirl Katherine Howard (as she then was) was always pressing her parents to tell her more about Frating.

The times were not propitious for such experiments, sandwiched as they were between two world wars, in a period of widespread poverty and unemployment; political and religious allegiances were tested to the point of breakdown. A number of the first generation of *Adelphi* supporters – Macmurray, Rees, Plowman and Brittain – had experienced the horrors of the Trenches at first hand, as had the fathers of Trevor Howard and the Barrett brothers. More than scriptural injunction, this is what had made them pacifists: they had experienced the charnel house of total war. As a working-class Christian pacifist during the First World War, Joe Watson had been handed a white feather; Peter Wells had been imprisoned for his beliefs at the outset of the Second World War. Trevor Howard's avowed pacificism was a matter to be negotiated with the Bishop of Chelmsford with regard to his ordination, and then in his application for a parish position, for which he had studied and desperately wished to achieve. On this matter the main issue concerned Howard's willingness to officiate at Remembrance Day services. According to his friend John Gibson, Howard agreed to take them 'but always arranged matters to avoid being associated with any military parades'. Likewise, from the formation of the Peace Pledge onwards, Vera Brittain had been excoriated in the press and verbally abused in the street and at meetings. In the early days of the Frating community, the children experienced these recriminations too.

A number of pacifists did change their minds on the limits of non-violence, mostly as a result of the Second World War and the grim struggle to defeat fascism, including very publicly the American theologian Rheinhold Niebuhr. Middleton Murry was another. In *Peace News* on 22 June 1945, shortly after VE Day, he admitted that:

> I misjudged two things. First I misjudged the nature of the average decent man, for whom non-violent resistance is infinitely more difficult and less natural than violent. The second mistake was even more serious. I gravely underestimated the terrible power of scientific terrorism as developed by the totalitarian police-states… I am therefore constrained in honesty to admit that under neither the Nazi nor the Soviet system of systematic and applied brutality does non-violent resistance stand a dog's chance… In a word, it seems to me that the scientific terrorism of the totalitarian police state – the wholesale reversion to medieval torture, with all the diabolical ingenuity of applied modern science – has changed the whole frame of reference within which modern pacifism was conceived.

In this Murry was adopting George Orwell's position, and here one can almost hear Orwell speaking. Ironically, Orwell himself had been rejected for military service when he attempted to enlist, and felt the rejection deeply. He had been someone who, according to Anthony Powell, 'saw himself as a man of action', and positively identified with military values. In the aftermath of the Second World War it was Orwell the novelist – no longer Tolstoy or Lawrence – who was creating the political weather for a post-war world, publishing *Animal Farm* in 1945 and Nineteen Eighty-Four in 1949. His are not novels of life or hope, but of disillusionment and fear, anticipating the destruction of the personal conscience as the overriding objective of totalitarianism and other forms of political oppression and social conformity. Everything Orwell touched was tinged with regret for failed idylls and ideals – whether that of rural England in *Coming Up for Air*, the defeat of the Republican government in the Spanish Civil War in *Homage to Catalonia*, or the idea of a socialist community, allegorised in *Animal Farm*. With regard to this last novel the historian W.H.G. Armytage was the first to suggest that this might have been partly inspired by Murry's experiences at Langham and then Theltenham:

> It is tempting to speculate whether George Orwell, who joined the original Adelphi summer school and who knew him well, found in the very shape of Murry's agrarian community, a hint for casting his own anti-Utopian *Animal Farm* as a farmyard story.

In 1954, eleven years after the group from Langham arrived at Frating Hall Farm, the Directors of the Frating Hall Farming Society called 'a Special Meeting of Members to decide whether the Society should carry on'. Feelings had come to a head regarding how far from the original spirit of the enterprise the management of the farm had strayed, as once again the Directors tried to balance the books from one difficult year to the next. This was made clear in the Directors' Statement to the members issued on 20 October 1954:

> It is recognised by all Directors that the Society has during recent years been moving away from its original concept of community and that little remains of this original ideal. The directors believe that members should decide whether in these circumstances they wish the Society to continue.

In many ways the farm's problems began almost as soon as the experiment started. Under-capitalised from the outset, the relatively small trading losses in the early years weighed the project down, which, together with a fall in property values, meant unless new capital investment was secured, the Society would go into liquidation, unable to pay its bills as they fell due or because the Society's assets were now worth less than its liabilities. New capital investment could only be sought if the Society rationalised the farm by employing a more conventional business model, reducing the wages bill, overheads and running costs. This, the majority of the Directors suggested, would be the only way of paying back the original members' shares. By this time there were 165 members of the Frating Hall Farm Society (only a small proportion of whom were living and working on the farm), each having invested money in the community. The Lamberts had put all their savings into the Frating Society as shares when they joined the community, and though they were eventually repaid, Phoebe Lambert told me, 'there was terrible ill-feeling because my parents got back, after ten years, exactly what they had put in'.

This was a bitter pill to swallow for everybody, made more distressing by the fact that 1954 had been a successful year at Frating with the farm now making a net profit. But with no sight in view of how the farm might pay back its historic debts as well as the original share capital, the Society was heading for the rocks. Five of the Directors were prepared to carry on, even to the extent of borrowing more money (one assumes on the basis of personal guarantees), but the three other Directors – Joe Watson, Donald Whitehouse and Fred Wickenden – were, according to the prospectus for the Special Meeting, 'no longer desirous of continuing as working members now that the original concept of community farming has disappeared'. The result was that the three left, more in sorrow than in anger.

Trevor and Enid Howard had already left Frating in 1952 in order that Trevor could train for ordination. In the letter to his daughter Katherine, written in 1962 in response to her asking about his memories of Frating, he gives a frank and generous account of why he thought the communal aspects of the project had proved so difficult:

> We wanted to found a pacifist, socialist and Christian community and demonstrate to the world that cooperation, and sharing could produce greater happiness and blessedness than individual strivings – that all you threw into the melting point would be returned to you sevenfold. We have learnt from other communities and from Langham that: i) there must be enough land to properly employ those in the community – the idea of ten working 6 acres, which some communities achieved seemed madness to us; ii) we believed that the married couples must have their own houses, although as it happened the marriages came before the houses and claims of different couples for what accommodation there was, was a great source of trouble; iii) we believed, in theory that the community should be democratically run – the farm by a management committee and the community by a general meeting. This too brought its quota of friction. After various forms of management had been tried the most successful long-term management of the farm came from the weekly farm tea which talked about the work for the next week – everyone on the management committee in other words, though of course Donald [Whitehouse] or Joe [Watson] as the heads of departments had to take day to day decisions.

Though Trevor admitted to his daughter that at times Joe had been 'too dictatorial and playing one chap, or family, off against one another', in the same sentence he repeated his belief that 'Joe made a terrific contribution to the social and cultural side which was really the finest fruit of the community'. Katherine told me that her father carried a photograph of Joe

Watson in his personal prayer book for the rest of his life.

Howard's reasons as to why he thought the project was unsustainable were all valid. Perhaps the most important was that at the outset the founding group were trying to achieve too many goals simultaneously, a number of which were potentially incompatible. It might be enough simply to be a pacifist in wartime, with all the pressures that would entail, but at the same time to live as a Christian, and as a socialist, while learning how to manage a farm from scratch and create a viable community out of a miscellaneous group of people who were similarly participating in the experiment from an equally wide variety of motives, was scaling Everest in a blizzard.

The important work in life continues

Martyn Thomas was still only ten when the cooperative project was dissolved, and could only look on as the adults and their families he had grown up with went their separate ways. Seventy-three years after arriving, he is still there, running Frating Hall Farm in partnership with his wife Barbara and their three sons and families. Martyn and Barbara remain fascinated by the story of the Frating Hall community – which he experienced at first hand – regarding it as a remarkable interlude in the history of Frating Hall, which has witnessed more than three centuries of life under changing owners and farming practices.

It was Martyn's stepfather Derek Crosfield who alone had the money to buy the farm after the cooperative venture was dissolved. Though Crosfield was another Langham and Frating pioneer, I wondered why he decided to take on the farm with all its financial obligations. Martyn told me that his stepfather hoped that he, Martyn, would eventually take it over and manage it in something like the spirit of the original project: as a Quaker, Crosfield had been genuinely committed to the Frating Hall community as first conceived. 'His Quakerism was a very important part of his life,' Barbara Thomas told me. Whilst still living at Frating, Crosfield became, successively, a Frating Parish Councillor, a Tendring District Councillor, an Essex County Councillor, and was to sit on many local government committees and hospital boards, while continuing to devote time to Quaker activities in the Colchester area. He was also involved with Christian Action Housing, and has a residential housing development in Clacton named after him. At the same time Martin's mother Marian Crosfield became involved with Amnesty and Oxfam in Colchester as well as pursuing her own arts projects. The important work in life continued.

After completing his studies at Writtle and undertaking two years' experience as a relief farmer, Martyn Thomas returned to Frating Hall Farm in 1966. After a lifetime of farming on the Tendring peninsula I asked him what the major changes in farming in that part of Essex had been in the period following the arrival of the Scots in the early part of the twentieth century, their decision to concentrate on dairy rather than wheat and other cereals. During and immediately after the Second World War, he said, 'you had to try anything, grow anything, the demand for any kind of food was relentless'. Over time, however, Essex had reverted to cereal farming because there was never really the right kind of grass pasture for livestock, and the famously dry weather of East Anglia helped restore its reputation as 'the bread-basket of England'. There were few big herds left in the county today, he thought, but the price of wheat had not increased for almost forty years, certainly since the 1980s. It is well known in farming circles that cereals are a bulk commodity, produced cheaply all over the world, and the only way it can be profitable for UK farmers to carry on is by increasing field size and employing larger and more sophisticated machinery.

The alternative is diversification. 'Diversification is huge,' he said, 'and farmers have to look out for any opportunity for income they can.'

When I asked why he thought the original cooperative project had run out of steam – he had obviously gleaned much about what had happened from his stepfather Derek over the years – Martyn thought that the principal issue to do with the running of any farm is the speed at which you have to respond to crises, large and small, as they happen. The care of livestock and tending crops in an ever-changing variety of weather conditions all have their own fast-moving routines and emergencies, none of which are amenable to forward planning, let alone daily collective deliberation on the allocation of duties. Basically, he said, 'if a job urgently needs doing at five in the morning, you can't wait for everybody to meet to decide who is going to do it'. Sometimes, Martyn added mischievously, 'you have to have a despot at the top'. Today many farms, including family farms, have professional farm managers to run them, he said, though that has been going on for a long time now. When Hugh Barrett left Frating with Deirdre to farm in Suffolk, he went initially as a manager, later conjuring up the idiosyncratic world of farm owners and their managers in his wonderfully detailed memoir, *A Good Living* – a book much admired and relished by Martyn and Barbara for the evocative picture it describes of traditional mixed farming in East Anglia before the age of agri-business and cereal monocultures arrived.

The 'New Life' and the post-war settlement

Yet though Orwell's England was a different and darker place than Lawrence's England, it was better in some ways too. Across war-ravaged Europe, the emphasis on post-war reconstruction had produced programmes for full employment, universal health provision and access to better education for all, not just in Britain. Social democracy was now at its zenith. The children of Frating belonged to this world and understandably took advantage of it, seeing the Britain of the 'post-war settlement' as a place where they could flourish and help others flourish too. And they did, as did many others of their – which is also my – generation.

Yet the instruments of change had themselves undergone a transformation. It was now the state that had appropriated the vision of the 'New Life' from the cradle to the grave, but this time planned and delivered from above. Furthermore, this required significantly less initiative or involvement from the beneficiaries themselves, despite the fact that they were paying for the welfare state through taxation. The philosophy of communitarianism advocated by Macmurray, Murry and others in the 1930s had given way to clientelism, no matter how well-meaning. In time public bureaucracies, sometimes unknowingly, sometimes not, undermined many of the long-standing forms of social solidarity and self-organisation. As a result, the friendly societies and 'mutuals', the cooperatives, the trade unions and the religious organisations – whose efforts state provision was originally intended to supplement or even enhance – were marginalised and sometimes completely bypassed. To use a phrase employed by one much-cited commentator on post-war cultural change, Richard Hoggart, the state had 'unbent the springs of action'.

To their credit, the Frating members could see this coming. In yet another letter from Trevor Howard to his future wife Enid Whitmore in January 1943, following Howard's participation in a WEA Brains Trust organised locally, he wrote that:

> The more I see of the pseudo-social service, local government, nursery schools, clinics, higher school leaving age socialism the more I incline to the gospel of Joe Watson, Middleton Murray, Max Plowman,

> Eric Gill and D.H. Lawrence – that what is needed is Life with a capital L – is red blood and honest sweat and adventure (Max used to say 'If you cannot sweat you will not live').

When we look back to the volatile political world of the 1930s, it is to be reminded of how much personal agency Christianity gave to its adherents – certainly from the evidence of the Langham and Frating circles. Though an atheist herself, the novelist and philosopher Iris Murdoch nevertheless devoted much thought to this question, both in her fiction and more discursive writing. In a seminal post-war collection of essays called *Convictions*, Murdoch's essay 'A House of Theory' concluded: 'Socialism no longer seems (as it seemed to certain favoured spirits) something essentially and profoundly Christian.' For her, politics had become detached from ethics, and she was preoccupied with the ontological issues raised by Christianity. Since then others have followed, most recently historian Tom Holland, another non-believer, who nevertheless in his book *Dominion* makes the bold assertion that Christianity is 'the most influential framework for making sense of human existence that has ever existed'. This may be disputed, but it probably held true across Europe until recently.

Re-reading Iris Murdoch's novel *The Bell*, I find the overlap between the world of Frating Hall Farm and Murdoch's fictional religious community compelling, if not surprising. Murdoch herself had been an *Adelphi* contributor, as noted before, she was interested in the early 1940s, reviewing books on Christian philosophy. She was interested in the ideas of the Russian Christian philosopher Nicholas Berdyaev, as were Murry and Watson. But it was in *The Bell* that she fully explored the complexities of religious belief when lived out in the day-to-day world of a working social community. These thoughts were confirmed when I was first told of that letter written in 1962 by Trevor Howard to daughter Katherine, still in her possession. In it he likened one of the farm collective meetings to those described in Murdoch's novel: 'I was most interested in Iris Murdoch's 'The Bell' how much their general meeting was like ours…' Likewise, Phoebe Lambert told me that her mother Joanna once told her, 'You must read *The Bell* – it's all about Frating!' Whether Murdoch had inside information, or impressive fictive intuition, she stands as an expert witness to the ways in which these complex social arrangements often unravelled.

Murdoch, already better known as a novelist than as a philosopher, had come to believe, as Lawrence had before her, that the novel – with its competing voices and characters in flux – was a more nuanced vehicle for representing the human condition than the academic treatise. 'We were interested in moral language, she was interested in the moral life,' her friend the philosopher Philippa Foot recalled. Though Lawrence is presently out of fashion as a novelist, one only has to go back to the poems and the letters (and, in my opinion, also the plays), to understand what all the fuss was about. One constant admirer amongst contemporary writers is novelist Rachel Cusk, who in her introduction to a new edition of *The Rainbow* draws out the sheer exhilarating energy of Lawrence's prose and 'why reading him remains a subversive, transformative, life-altering act'. In his wonder, and his passionate and emotional response to the world, to people, to places and perhaps particularly to the natural world, especially to animals, there was never another writer like him: only John Berger perhaps comes near. Both were freely at ease in a variety of forms, whether as novelists, poets, artists, essayists, travel writers and critics, and with both writers you never knew what was coming next. The critic Geoff Dyer supports this comparison, observing that with Berger as with Lawrence, 'One is always aware of him looking. He is like Lawrence in his pyjamas at the water trough on that hot, hot day, waiting for something interesting to happen.' Dyer is alluding here to Lawrence's great poem 'Snake'.

On matters of religious belief and morality again, even an intellectual sceptic and religious agnostic such as the late Edward Said was prepared to appreciate the revolutionary ethic at the heart of the Christian faith. For it was a religion, he once wrote, which uniquely 'shatters the balance between high and low styles, just as Jesus' life destroys the separation between the sublime and the everyday'. As a fluid, humanist ontology, Christianity, though ostensibly transcendental, seemed to allow for both piety and direct political action, and for individual redemption as well as collective self-determination. In short, it had practical outcomes as well as possessing an immanent spirituality. Anybody who today claimed that the Labour Party still owes more to Methodism than Marxism, or that the Church of England remains substantively the Conservative Party at prayer – views once commonly held and thought to determine the relationship between politics and religion in Britain – would be heard with bemusement.

Similarly, those believing that Quakerism has always been a uniquely quietist form of religious observance need to realise just how active the Quakers were in those days, and not only in the anti-war movement. They were active in international refugee campaigns, in social welfare provision, local government politics and in those difficult times of the 1930s – through the unusual circumstances of the 'reserved occupations' – in the farming community. Such beliefs continued to overlap with the Tolstoyan ethos that what mattered most was not what you believed but how you lived your life. It is 'life' once again that is the organising principle of these endeavours, with, in John Middleton Murry's words, 'more life' being the end point of political action.

What was further unexpected in the story of Langham and Frating was the increased convergence between pacifism and agrarianism. This was evident in Max Plowman's role at the Peace Pledge Union's Forethought Committee, which had argued for pacifists to take up farming projects, though *The Adelphi* had expressed 'back-to-the-land' sentiments and ambitions from the beginning. In an essay on the history of that journal, critic Michael H. Whitworth wrote that 'By the 1940s, the journal was calling for a national renaissance based on an agricultural renaissance, a position derived from Murry's pacifism.' But Murry had been arguing for this position since the 1920s, and to the end of his life retained a strong belief in the redemptive power of farming. And in a letter to T.S. Eliot written on 14 May 1945, he stated that 'I am convinced that if a country has enough imagination to get its agriculture right, it will get everything else right – or not wholly wrong.'

In this regard it is worth repeating that though Murry regrettably came to be disliked by many of those who worked with him – doubtless contributing to the fact that his reputation today is at a very low ebb – this was largely caused by his chaotic personal and financial affairs. In his lifetime many significant writers and intellectuals, particularly those not directly involved with his business and practical schemes, continued to regard him as an important political and religious figure, and a force for good. T.S. Eliot, for example, who certainly did not suffer fools gladly, maintained a thoughtful and engaged friendship with Murry until the latter's death.

Unfinished business

The Langham and Frating idealists were not alone in believing that history might have a final destination to which humanity was heading in the search for social perfectibility. Such dreams didn't only have their origins in nineteenth-century theories of political economy promulgated by heavily bearded men, but have been part and parcel of a much longer tradition of imagined new worlds promised by religious and political ideologies, whether enshrined in films, fiction and poetry, or modelled in architecture, urban planning, formalised gardens ('nature perfected!') and human landscapes. In the case of the last, utopian thinking has left a more lasting impression, whether as idealised settlements or even whole cities – as well as ruins.

The Frating Hall community was initially imagined as a pastoral idyll, the final destination of what Joe Watson described as 'the journey to our hearts' desire'. Yet with the prior experience of the difficulties at Langham there was a much greater realism about what could be achieved. With lessons learned in the first eighteen months, the fact is that by the time the 1946 report 'Three Years A-Growing' was printed and distributed, they were able to tell a story not of failed dreams but of hard-won success.

We have to be wary of calling Frating a utopian experiment: it was in reality a thoroughly practical experiment in establishing and managing a working farm whilst living communally. When W.H.G. Armytage's wide-ranging history of utopian communities *Heavens Below* was published in 1962, fellow-historian J.F.C. Harrison praised the book's scholarship, but warned against the dangers of defining the term 'utopian' too broadly. One can only do damage to the concept, Harrison argued, if Sir Thomas More's fictional Utopia, Robert Owen's paternalistic industrial community at New Lanark and twentieth-century planning models such as Welwyn Garden City are all lumped in together – even if all are admirable in their own way. There is a difference, he argued, between a utopian dream and an experiment in living differently.

Too often, Harrison wrote, historians treat such experiments or fictional exercises as marginal, because they are nearly always seen to 'fail'. Yet in truth, experiments cannot fail – it is inherent in their function to try something and see what happens, not to achieve a preordained result. As Katherine Weaver told me, 'so much of these endeavours are simply unfinished business'. The Frating Hall Farming Society was, it is more accurate to say, a social experiment. We learn from experiments so that we can conduct them again, under different conditions, employing other variables: they are reflexive. The experimental mode is a mode through which new ideas can be developed and discoveries are made. The difference between a social experiment and an attempt to create a utopia is not one of gradation but of kind.

On such questions there is a salutary exchange in Turgenev's elegiac novel of rural life *Fathers and Sons*, regarding the recurring conflict between hope in the present and hope for the future. It occurs when the kindly estate-owner and farmer Nikolai Kirsanov takes issue with the young nihilist Yevgeny Bazarov: 'You're condemning everything or, to be more precise, you're pulling everything down, but surely you've got to build something as well.' 'That's not for us to do,' Bazarov responds. 'First we've got to clear the ground.' At Frating Hall they cleared the ground, sometimes almost literally, and for a while, under difficult circumstances, created a viable self-sufficient community, the lineaments of which remain in the preserved Hall, barn and granary, in the cottages they built, and the striking lime-tree avenue.

William Wordsworth knew these dilemmas well. In this instance it is the late-eighteenth-century Lakeland poet writing, not his descendant who spent time at Frating. In Book XI of 'The Prelude' – reflecting on his time in revolutionary France – the poet concluded that those seeking contentment should search:

Not in Utopia, subterranean fields,
Or some secreted island, Heaven knows where!
But in the very world, which is the world
Of all of us,—the place where in the end
We find our happiness, or not at all!

In much the same spirit, the late Colin Ward, astute chronicler of arcadian settlements, was fond of citing Alexander Herzen's premonitory warning against utopian millennialism: 'A goal which is infinitely remote is not a goal at all, it is a deception.' There is a value in utopian visions, but they are visions not programmes. The Frating pioneers were concerned not with how they might live in the future, but how they might live now. The dangers of investing too much trust in the future recalls a joke I was told many years ago in Sweden. Sven tells Per that he has a new job, standing on a plinth looking out for the coming revolution. How much, asks Per? 50 kroner a day. That's not much, Per says. It's a lifetime's work, says Sven. For the community at Frating, life on the farm was about what needed to be done today, not tomorrow. 'We did not wait,' Joe Watson once wrote, 'because there was nothing to wait for.'

The land is all over the place

For people with little direct experience of farming, change only becomes apparent when the countryside begins to look (or smell) differently, or when they notice things have gone missing: birdsong, flocks of lapwings, hares, wildflowers, hedgerows, elms, pigs, ducks and chickens, and people working the land. Seen from the air, East Anglia today is a formal patchwork quilt of yellow and green squares – largely devoid of life. What adds to this sense of absence is that, in the bleak, prophetic words of Nan Fairbrother's seminal work *New Lives, New Landscapes* – from which this chapter takes its title – 'the animals have gone indoors'. The loss of flora and fauna in the English countryside has been devastating, and for this, many believe, modern farming practices are to blame.

The visual changes were noted by The Countryside Agency some years ago in a report *Agricultural Landscapes: 33 Years of Change*, including photographs showing 'before' and 'after' images of scenes from rural Britain over nearly two generations. Of all the regions studied, East Anglia had changed the most:

> The perception at the time that the study started in the early 1970s was that the major arable areas of East Anglia were the areas where maximum change had taken place; that in those areas it had gone too far and was greatly damaging in both broad amenity and in wildlife terms.

The explanation as to why East Anglia had changed so significantly was the predominance of cereals. With the price subject to intense international market competition, as Martyn Thomas observed, only the single-minded rationalisation of farming could keep farming going in the region. To his credit Middleton Murry had seen this coming, though whether he – or anybody else in fact – had the answer as to how to reconcile the economic sustainability of British agriculture with environmental sustainability, remains the great unresolved problem. In his late-in-life memoir Murry wrote:

> Finally, in spite of the zealous advocates of throwing field into field and farm into farm to make modern latifundia worked by gangs of specialized workers, few honest observers believe that agricultural production (as distinct from individual profit) will thereby be increased. The consensus of informed opinion is that, on the whole, the existing system of moderate-sized farms is the best for getting the best out of the land of England.

Whether this is true or not, others better qualified will say. What I had not realised until studying the history of the farm at Frating was just how variegated in its geology, soil type and suitability for arable and/or livestock even a medium-sized family farm of 300 acres could be. As we have seen, the farm sat on an extraordinary mixture of alluvium, gravel, brick earth, London clay and sand, varying in quality from one field to the next, which the Frating farmers only realised once they began farming in earnest. Nothing is simple when it comes to the land or the weather.

Martyn Thomas put the matter more simply. 'DEFRA,' he told me, 'classifies agricultural land into four categories: Grades 1–4. Here at Frating we have some Grade 1, but it is mostly Grades 2 and 3.' You make the most of what you can. For all his faults, Middleton Murry had his own understanding of these matters, even if his organisational skills were not up to taking advantage of these insights:

> It may be granted that the pattern of British agriculture is largely imposed by the nature of the land itself. The land is, thank goodness, all over the place; and there it will remain. The land of Britain is full of idiosyncrasy. Nothing like the equivalent of the homogenous American or Russian prairie is to be found in Britain. On most British farms, the characteristics of one field differ remarkably from those of another: they have to be studied and humoured.

Murry had the studiousness, but sadly lacked the humour. Or so those who worked with him said.

'No smooth road into the future'

The future of farming in Britain, and of the countryside itself, echoes a remark made in the novel *The Leopard* by Giuseppe Tomasi di Lampedusa, a story taking place when political upheaval and an emboldened capitalism threatens the old way of life in Sicily. Its hero reflects that: 'For everything to stay the same, everything must change.' In order to restore the richness and diversity of flora and fauna found in the countryside before industrialised farming took hold, and to foster easier access for small farmers to land and markets whilst bringing back the orchards and local traditions of food production, it is clear that there needs to be a revolution in attitudes and agrarian practices.

Complicating this process is the problem of 'shifting baseline syndrome': when exactly was the British countryside at its most biodiverse and beautiful, let alone most productive? Each generation tends to remember the environment of their childhood as the baseline for what is right and proper, before it all went wrong. The cultural critic Raymond Williams devotes the early part of his seminal book *The Country and the City* to detailing the never-ending melancholic complaint of each generation as being the last to witness the 'real' countryside: an endless processional of anxiety that reaches back to Virgil. It is there still in the latest evocation of 'traditional farming'– James Rebanks' otherwise passionate and forward-looking disquisition *English Pastoral*: 'I was a boy living through the last days of an ancient farming world,' he writes at the outset. But the countryside has been declining – and also renewing – for millennia, though in terms of biodiversity we are almost certainly at a low point right now.

One persuasive voice amongst those promoting countryside renewal is that of economist Dieter Helm. In *Green and Prosperous Land: A Blueprint for Rescuing the British Countryside*, Helm frames environmental renewal within the classical economic models of public goods, private goods, open markets and hard-headed bottom-line results, finding some kind of equilibrium in between. Suspicious of economists who come bearing good news, I was reassured to learn that one of Helm's grandfathers had himself farmed 350 acres on the Essex marshes close to the River Blackwater – coincidentally at the same time as the Frating Hall community were at work. Helm remembered his grandfather's farm as a 'mixed dairy and arable farm, with traditional farmyard chickens and ducks, a big vegetable garden, a small orchard and of course beehives'. In middle age he has decided to use his economic insights to see if he can return British agriculture to something like that pastoral idyll, having seen the hedges of his grandfather's traditional farm dynamited to oblivion and the 350 acres turned into a single field in the 1960s after the title was sold.

Farmers will not be pleased with Helm's own economic baselines. He refers on several occasions to the fact that agriculture now only contributes 1 per cent to the UK's GDP, whereas tourism contributes 10 per cent, concluding that the biodiversification and beautification of the countryside is more important economically than agricultural intensification in the name of food security. For agri-business this is fighting talk. But Helm is persuasive:

> The danger here is that the countryside becomes a picture-postcard theme park rather than being recognised as a working environment – but perhaps we should see leisure and tourism as being part of that working environment, and, importantly, a part that helps to safeguard it.

Yet even if Helm doesn't say so explicitly, the implication of his argument is that the issue of food security – that is to say whether the UK can ever become self-reliant on food, or indeed whether this is desirable let alone necessary – is something to be discussed on another occasion, though it is a question that the Covid-19 pandemic has raised anew. He is not overly worried that we need to import 40 per cent of our food, given that much of it takes the form of fruit, vegetables, spices, teas, coffees and wines that cannot be grown or produced easily at home, though with global heating this proposition itself may be redundant soon.

Helm's foresight chimes in with the work of another East Anglian with farming roots, Marina O'Connell, mentioned earlier regarding her involvement with the Land Settlement Association. Describing herself as having 'come from seven generations of Dutch nurserymen, from the small village of Boskoop in the Netherlands, famous for its fruit tree "Belle of Boskoop"', she and her husband established The Apricot Centre at Lawford, just eight miles from Frating, nearly twenty years ago: a four-acre woodland, orchard, teaching centre and market garden run on organic farming principles. As O'Connell relates in her forthcoming book *A Toolkit of Sustainable Food Systems*, the site they took over,

> matured from a flat, ordinary oblong of depleted pasture, and then something rather magical happened. It became very abundant, the food tasted delicious, it was and still is full of wildlife. We had Sparrowhawks, Turtle doves, Grass snakes, Owls, Foxes, Elephant Hawkmoths, the dawn chorus was a racket. It was then that I really knew that these systems worked extremely well.

The success of the Centre led them to being invited by Martin Large of the Biodynamic Land Trust to put in a proposal for a new 13-hectare bare-field site, 'a miserable little bit of land', on the edge of Dartington Hall Estate in Totnes, previously farmed with little thought to its long-term future. The couple took possession of Huxhams Cross Farm in 2015, purchased by the Trust with the help of 150 shareholders – much the same as the Frating Hall arrangement – and is now a fully operational biodynamic farm. It grows and sells a wide range of vegetables, as well as chickens, eggs and wheat, and, as importantly, is also home to a thriving well-being service for young people and families. The soil has been transformed after three years of sustainable farming practices following forty years of industrial barley crops. Like Frating, Huxhams Cross Farm has a social agenda as well as an agricultural purpose – but this may become a feature of all farming in the future. For as James Rebanks, the writer-farmer cited above, has said on more than one occasion: 'Feeding people is a noble endeavour.'

Nobody expects an immediate counter-revolution in farming, in which large agri-business operations are forcibly returned to small, organic homesteads and landholdings. Yet the demand for a new appreciation of farming is again being heard, another consequence of the Covid-19 pandemic. Issues of food availability and quality were brought to the fore as a result of the pandemic, with 'lockdown' witnessing a 400-per-cent rise in subscription 'box' schemes, by which farmers deliver directly to people's homes. An added cause for anxiety is the prospect of post-Brexit trade deals threatening to water down, if not tear up, animal-welfare standards as well as environmental consideration. It further appears that the cheapness of food, rather than its quality, will become a major factor in future trade negotiations between the UK and the rest of the world. Such worries have been forcefully expressed by Rebanks:

> A civilisation or a society that doesn't look after its countryside, doesn't look after its soil, doesn't look after its food supply, let alone its nature, is a deeply irresponsible and flawed society. The idea that we would agree to American trade demands to take 'place of origin' off food labelling, so you won't know where it comes from, and that would outlaw any kind of environmental payments to farmers so that we could do things better – and if I'm really honest I think we need higher environmental standards in this country – then we don't need a trade deal that puts enormous pressures on farmers to make things worse.

> The proposed American trade deal is arguably the most disastrous thing proposed for the countryside for the last fifty, maybe hundred, years.

This is why the story of Frating Hall Farm is compelling. It reminds us that food issues can bring farming and wider social and environmental concerns together, particularly in a time of crisis. It is the sovereign domain of the farm and smallholding that provides an appropriate vehicle for exploring these issues. And here we come to the main problem. For as James Rebanks makes clear: 'The marginalisation of farming in our national politics and culture is a tragedy because this is all about the kind of country we want to live in.' Writer Melissa Harrison endorses this perspective for different reasons, observing that farming is still regarded as being outside the concerns of those interested in the natural world:

> We've got a blind spot in this country when it comes to farming and agricultural landscapes, and I see that in nature writing, which is such a popular field, and yet farmland is almost entirely absent from it.

Wrapped up in the farm question are pressing issues of environmental sustainability, the restoration of biodiversity to the countryside, animal welfare, food quality, local economic development, public health and, with luck, improved understanding between town and country. Unwrap farming and you unwrap almost everything to do with human society and the natural world.

Yet as Lawrence declared in the opening paragraph of *Lady Chatterley's Lover*, there is no smooth road into the future. There is something prescient about the pre-war enthusiasm for the writings of D.H. Lawrence – with their hopes for a new life of 'new little habitats' and 'new little hopes' – being supplanted by George Orwell's bleak prospect for the future, under an all-seeing and all-powerful centralised

The barn at Frating today.

state. How could two such entirely different visions coexist given both had their intellectual origins in the same 'Adelphi' political and cultural milieu? The differences between the two writers is not as substantial as commonly assumed. Both *Lady Chatterley's Lover* and *Nineteen Eighty-Four* – the novels which brought their authors their greatest fame or notoriety – were written by men whose short lives were long foreshadowed by tuberculosis. In an extraordinary coincidence, critic Michael Ross discovered that Orwell's medical consultant Dr Andrew Morland was the very same man who had treated Lawrence, twenty years earlier. Yet despite their contrasting aesthetic ambitions, Ross is surely right to say that between them they produced 'the two English novels of our century that have had the most decided impact on the general public's habits of thinking'. Each in their own way created what Raymond Williams termed a new 'structure of feeling': one guardedly optimistic, the other profoundly pessimistic. And there is one more similarity. In Lawrence's lifelong wish to recapture the happiness he had once felt in Eastwood, and in Orwell's decision to locate his lost or subverted Eden, it is the iconic setting of a family farm – Hagg's Farm near Eastwood for Lawrence, the allegorical Manor Farm in *Animal Farm* for Orwell – which is used as a framing device to explore 'the condition of England' question. To paraphrase anthropologist Claude Lévi-Strauss, farms are good to think with.

When D.H. Lawrence and John Middleton Murry first dreamed of establishing their ideal community, they envisaged a place of fellowship and mutual love, requiring a complete revolution in personal relations. Yet the two men lacked a deeper understanding of the kind of settlement, as well as its social and economic underpinnings, which might allow such relations to prosper. At the back of his mind, Murry's model was almost certainly some kind of monastic retreat or prelapsarian idyll, for which God or some other deity would provide.

It is to Murry's credit – and one of the more impressive qualities of this quixotic, intellectually gifted, volatile, unhappy man – that he was quick to understand that a moral counterweight to militarism could be advanced through the cultivation of the land. Where Orwell foresaw the future as a barracks or prison, Murry, like Lawrence, hoped to find its best realisation in the shape of a farm. If Murry stayed true to just one overriding principle in his life – given that his personal religious and political interests and affiliations strayed to all points of the compass over time – it was in the duty towards the land. 'Work on the land,' we are reminded in *Community Farm*, 'is necessary to the life of man in a way that no other work can be. I believe that service to the land is an unconditional good.' On this matter he remains a visionary, as do the earnest group of people who, sharing an abhorrence of war, threw their lot in together, laboured in the fields, cared for the animals, kept an eye out for each other's children, foraged in the woods, entertained visitors and refugees, sang in choirs and took their chances in life as members of the Frating Hall Farm Society. The evidence of their letters, conversations, diaries, reminiscences and other archive records, only confirms – as writer Fernando Pessoa profoundly suggested – that in the writing of such histories, what was felt is what was lived.

Hand-carved sign for Frating Hall Farm
by Mark Harvey.

Notes

Further details of all books can be found in the *Bibliography.*

INTRODUCTION

The *Radical Essex* book, edited by Hayley Dixon and Joe Hill, is published by Focal Point Gallery. It was based the exhibition of the same name held at the gallery in 2016, and also featured talks and walks across the county. Essays by Tim Burrows, Charles Holland, Gillian Darley, Jules Lubbock, Jess Twyman, Rachel Lichtenstein, Catherine Hyland and myself covered all aspects of social and political life, architecture and landscape in the twentieth century, including maps, photographs and hiking and cycling itineraries.

Le Grand Meaulnes by Alain-Fournier is one of the indispensable and most magical novels of the twentieth century. Published in 1913, a year before the death of the author in the First World War, it is a story of adolescent longing for love, based on a chance encounter at a mysterious house hidden deep in rural France.

CHAPTER ONE

The clearest account of the proposed Lawrence/Murry communal household at Zennor can be found in Murry's memoir *Between Two Worlds* (1935). Lawrence's letter to Lady Asquith is cited in Dennis Hardy's encyclopaedic study *Utopian England*, a vital source book for this chapter and others.

Murry's relationship with both his wife Katherine Mansfield and D.H. Lawrence is detailed in Murry's daughter's memoir *Beloved Quixote*, though it is, understandably, partisan.

Frank Lea's biography *The Life of John Middleton Murry*

combines sympathy with acute awareness of Murry's many failings, whilst acknowledging Murry's considerable intellectual range and influence.

A.N. Wilson's biography of Tolstoy is especially helpful on Tolstoy's enthusiastic readership in Britain, where his disciples cultivated a devoted following.

I was lucky in having Victor Gray's definitive account of Tolstoy's followers in Essex published in 2019: *A New World in Essex*.

The story of the 'Redeeming Scots' who allegedly rescued Essex farming in the early decades of the twentieth century is told by E.H. Hunt and S.J. Pam in the *Agricultural History Review*, detailed in the bibliography.

Most of what I learned about the Land Settlement Association (LSA) came from Marina O'Connell, herself a former smallholder in north-east Essex. She develops some of the lessons learned in her important forthcoming book *A Toolkit of Sustainable Food Systems* (2021).

CHAPTER TWO

Joe Watson's short but generous memoir of Murry, 'A Good Workman and his Friends: Recollections of John Middleton Murry' was published by the *London Magazine* in 1959, following Murry's death.

George Woodcock's accounts of Langham are all taken from Dennis Hardy's book cited above. Though George Woodcock (1912–1995) found the Langham experiment disenchanting, he nevertheless remained wholly committed, as an anarchist and a pacifist, to farming projects. Born in Canada, he came to England as a child with his parents, refused to go to Cambridge University, became a railway worker and subsequently a prolific writer on political matters. He was a friend of Herbert Read, and after an early public disagreement with Orwell they too became close friends, and Woodcock's biography of Orwell *The Crystal Spirit: A Study of George Orwell*, published in 1966, is indispensable.

Vera Brittain's memories of Langham and Frating can be found in *Testament of Experience*, and the story of her pacifism fully explored by Muriel Melldown in her essay listed in the bibliography. I am also indebted to *Vera Brittain: A Life* by Paul Berry and Mark Bostridge.

I am grateful to Barbara and Martyn Thomas for providing a copy of the extremely moving collection of stories by conscientious objectors in the Colchester area, including those of Hugh Clunes and Bill Skinner: a limited photocopied edition, produced and distributed by the 'Friends of Colchester and Coggeshall Monthly Meeting', edited by Charles Blather.

CHAPTER THREE

Murry's indispensable account of his many and varied attempts to establish farming communities was written and published near the end of his life and is one of his happier books: *Community Farm*, published in 1953, with delightful line drawings by Richard Murry.

There are many brief accounts of the famous 1936 Adelphi Summer School, some contradictory, and I have tried to harmonise all the different versions. There is also much confusion as to when and where the other summer schools were held. The first was held in 1934 at Glossop, the second in 1935 at Caerlon, the third in 1936 at Langham, and the fourth and last in 1937 at Murry's home at The Old Rectory, Larling, in Norfolk.

John Costello's *John Macmurray: A Biography* is a richly rewarding book about a complex and impressive philosopher and public intellectual, whose reputation is on the rise again.

Amateur theatre thrived in the first half of the twentieth century, very much as a community and socially conscious affair. Peter Billingham's study *Theatres of Conscience 1939–1953* is strongly recommended.

Iris Murdoch's novel *The Bell*, when read in tandem with the story of Frating Hall Farm, only adds to the wonder and fragility of such experiments in human redemption.

Frank Lea remains the mystery man of this story. Though he was a prolific writer, poet, theologian and philosopher, and good friend of Frating, I have been unable to find out any more about him apart from a brief obituary by Middleton Murry in *The Times* announcing his 'sudden death': a customary phrase implying Lea took his own life.

One of the unexpected pleasures of researching this book was to be recommended a book as then unknown to me: Hugh Barrett's exquisite memoir of farming in Suffolk *A Good Living*. I am grateful to his son John Barrett for leading me to this book, but also for making a present to me of Hugh's own copy of Frank Lea's biography of Middleton Murry, dedicated to Hugh by Lea himself. Now much treasured.

The difficult, sometimes acrimonious, exchange of letters between Murry and Joe Watson, as the Langham project unravels and the two decide to go separate ways, is painfully recorded in dozens of letters between them kept by Watson's daughter Joan and which the family kindly made available.

CHAPTER FOUR

Much of this chapter is based on interviews, conversations and exchanges of letters with John Barrett, Phoebe Lambert, Janice Smith (née Watson) and Katherine Weaver (née Howard), to whom I am deeply grateful.

For the story of Benton End (formally known as the East Anglian School of Painting and Drawing), a good starting point is *Benton End Remembered*, compiled and edited by Gwynneth Reynolds and Diana Grace. This old farmhouse and extensive gardens in Hadleigh, Suffolk, was for over forty years a gathering place for artists, writers and gardeners, and is remembered fondly in this collection of reminiscences by former students.

After leaving Frating, Roderic Barrett went on to become a successful painter, whose life and work is the subject of David Buckman's illustrated study *Roderic Barrett* (2003).

Joe Watson's son Peter Watson published a memoir of his own childhood at Frating under the title *Community Farm Boyhood*, detailed in the bibliography.

CHAPTER FIVE

This chapter is almost wholly dependent on interviews and conversations with Jan Smith, Kate Weaver, Barbara and Martyn Thomas, Hugh Barrett and Phoebe Lambert, together with the letters and other archive material they generously provided.

Much of the detail of the farm's landholdings, crops and stockholdings are contained in two published reports: 'Three Years A-Growing', Annual Report, Frating Hall Farm, March 1946 and 'Frating Hall Community', undated pamphlet, circa 1948/49.

If I had to take only ten books to a desert island, two would be by the historian Keith Thomas: *Man and the Natural World* and *Religion and the Decline of Magic*. No understanding of everyday English life and culture – especially rural life – over the past four hundred years is possible without them.

CHAPTER SIX

In addition to Peter Billingham's history *Theatres of Conscience*, mentioned in Chapter three, the story of Mary Kelly's intrepid support for amateur theatre – particularly religious theatre – in the first half of the twentieth century is told in Andrew Walker's essay 'The "Uncertainty of Our Climate": Mary Kelly and Rural Theatre', in *Rural Modernity in Britain*, edited by Kristin Bluemel and Michael McCluskey.

Particular thanks to Martyn Thomas and Peter Watson for their written and recorded testimony used in this chapter.

Trevor Howard's proposed WEA class provided the inspiration for my appendix: 'Prophets of a New World'.

Max Plowman's letters are always interesting, and a good collection is *Bridge into the Future*, published in 1944 after his death and edited by his widow Dorothy Plowman.

The composer William Wordsworth (1908–1988), himself a conscientious objector, became a close friend of many of the Frating members, often visiting the farm. He is the composer of eight symphonies, six string quartets and many other works, and his work is still being performed and recorded today.

The best single-volume biography of D.H. Lawrence is that by John Worthen, *D.H. Lawrence: The Life of an Outsider*.

CHAPTER SEVEN

All details of Frating Farm's geology, soil types and topology are contained in the two reports mentioned in Chapter Four: 'Three Years A-Growing', Annual Report, Frating Hall Farm, March 1946 and 'Frating Hall Community', undated pamphlet, circa 1948/49.

Writtle College in Chelmsford, Essex, is one of the largest and oldest agricultural colleges in the UK, and has always enjoyed considerable prestige in the farming world. Briefly associated with Essex University for degree purposes, it was granted university status in its own right in 2017, and is now known as Writtle University College.

As with Dennis Hardy's book *Utopian Britain*, *Heavens Below: Utopian Experiments in England 1560–1960*, by W.H.G. Armytage, is indispensable.

Particular thanks to Barbara and Martyn Thomas for providing me with much of the detail of Frating Hall Farm today, and for current farming issues in East Anglia and beyond.

The comments by Melissa Harrison and James Rebanks were made on the BBC Radio 4 programme *Start the Week*, devoted to the future of farming, and first broadcast on Monday 31 August 2020.

Bibliography and sources

ARCHIVE DOCUMENTS

'Christmas Letter', Joe Watson, December 1945

'Three Years A-Growing', Annual Report, Frating Hall Farm, March 1946

'Frating Hall Community', undated pamphlet, circa 1948/49

'Written about 1951', typescript by Phyllis Marian Crosfield

'COs Reminiscences, Stories by Friends of Colchester and Coggleshall Monthly Meeting', edited by Charles Bather

Map of the farm and field system kindly supplied by Barbara and Martyn Thomas

'A Brief Chronicle of the Life of Trevor Howard', typescript by John Gibson, 1989, kindly supplied by Katherine Weaver

'On Being Hungry', J.H. Watson, typescript for BBC Radio talk in March 1955

'A Note about Joe Watson', typescript by Sid Chaplin, kindly supplied by Jan Smith

Sixty-six letters from John Middleton Murry to Joe Watson, 1937–1952

Seventeen letters from Max Plowman to Joe Watson, 1937–1941, kindly supplied by Joanna Dunn, Pat Smith and Adam Smith

(It was with great sadness that I learned of Joanna Dunn's death in September 2020 at the age of eighty-eight.)

PHOTOGRAPHS

I am grateful for the use of photographs supplied by John Barrett, Paul Burrow, Phoebe Lambert, Jan Smith, Barbara and Martyn Thomas, Katherine Weaver and the family of the late Joanna Dunn. Contemporary photographs were taken by Larraine Worpole and Ken Worpole.

BOOKS

Arjakovsky, Antoine, 2014, *The Way: Religious Thinkers of the Russian Emigration in Paris and Their Journal, 1925–1940*, University of Notre Dame Press, Notre Dame, IN.

Armytage, W.H.G., 1961, *Heavens Below: Utopian Experiments in England 1560–1960*, Routledge and Kegan Paul, London.

Barrett, Hugh, 2002, *A Good Living*, Old Pond Publishing, Ipswich.

Berry, Paul and Bostridge, Mark, 1995, *Vera Brittain: A Life*, Chatto and Windus, London.

Billingham, Peter, 2000, *Theatres of Conscience, 1939–53: A Study of Four Touring British Community Theatre Groups*, Routledge, London.

Brittain, Vera, 1980, *Testament of Experience*, Fontana, London.

Buckman, David, 2003, *Roderic Barrett*, Chappel Galleries, Colchester, Essex.

Chambers, Emma, 2016, *Paul Nash*, Tate Publishing, London.

Colls, Robert, 2013, *George Orwell: English Rebel*, Oxford University Press, Oxford.

Costello, John E., 2002, *John Macmurray: A Biography*, Floris Books, Edinburgh.

Cusk, Rachel, 2011, 'Introduction', *The Rainbow* by D.H. Lawrence, Vintage Books, London.

Darley, Gillian, 2019, *Excellent Essex*, Old Street Publishing, London.

Davison, Peter Hobley (editor), 2000, *George Orwell: Collected Works, A Kind of Compulsion 1903–1936*, Vol. 10, Secker and Warburg, London.

Emmet, Alfred, 'Amateur Theatre', in *The Continuum*

Companion to Twentieth-Century Theatre, edited by Colin Chambers, Continuum, London, 2002.

Everitt, Eileen, 2007, *The Development of Lower Mayland and Maylandsea during the 20th Century*, self-published.

Fairbrother, Nan, 1970, *New Lives, New Landscapes*, Architectural Press, London.

Field, John, 2013, *Working Men's Bodies*, Manchester University Press, Manchester.

Gray, Victor, 2019, *A New World in Essex: The Rise and Fall of the Purleigh Brotherhood Colony, 1896–1903*, Campanula Books, Wivenhoe, Essex.

Hardy, Dennis, 2000, *Utopian England: Community Experiments 1900–1945*, E and FN Spon, London.

Harris, Alexandra, 2010, *Romantic Moderns*, Thames and Hudson, London.

Heppenstall, Rayner, 1988, *Four Absentees*, Sphere, London.

Jones, Tobias, 2007, *Utopian Dreams: A Search for a Better Life*, Faber, London.

Lambert, Phoebe, 2011, *Dark Shadow, Bright Sun*, AuthorHouse, Bloomington, IN.

Lea, F.A., 1948, *The Seed of the Church*, Sheppard Press, London.

Lea, F.A., 1959, *The Life of John Middleton Murry*, Methuen, London.

Lea, F.A., 1962, *A Defence of Philosophy*, Eyre and Spottiswoode, London.

Markus, Thomas A., 1993, *Buildings and Power: Freedom and Control in the Origin of Modern Building*, Routledge, London.

Marsh, Jan, 1982, *Back to the Land*, Quartet Books, London.

Murry, John Middleton, 1935, *Between Two Worlds*, Jonathan Cape, London.

Murry, John Middleton, 1953, *Community Farm*, The Country Book Club, London.

Murry Middleton, Katherine, 1986, *Beloved Quixote*, Souvenir Press, London.

O'Connell, Marina, forthcoming 2021, *A Toolkit of Sustainable Food Systems*, Hawthorn Press, Stroud.

Plowman, Max, 1942, *The Right to Live*, Andrew Dakers Ltd, London.

Rebanks, James, 2015, *The Shepherd's Life*, Allen Lane, London.

Rebanks, James, 2020, *English Pastoral*, Allen Lane, London.

Rees, Richard, 1958, *Brave Men: A Study of D.H. Lawrence and Simone Weil*, Gollancz, London.

Reynolds, Gwynneth and Grace, Diana, 2002, *Benton End Remembered*, Unicorn Press, London.

Saunders, Hetty, 2017, *My House of Sky: The Life and Work of J.A. Baker*, Little Toller Books, Dorset.

Taylor, D.J., 2003, *Orwell*, Chatto and Windus, London.

Thomas, Keith, 1984, *Man and the Natural World*, Penguin Books, London.

The Countryside Agency, 2006, *Agricultural Landscapes: 33 Years of Change*, The Countryside Agency, Cheltenham, Glos.

Wallerstein, Immanuel, 1998, *Utopistics: Or, Historical Choices of the Twenty-First Century*, The New Press, New York.

Watson, Peter, 2014, *Community Farm Boyhood*, Outskirts Press, Parker, Colorado, USA.

Williams, Raymond, 1975, *The Country and the City*, Granada, St Albans.

Williams, Shirley, 2009, *Climbing the Bookshelves*, Virago, London.

Wilson, A.N., 2012, *Tolstoy*, Atlantic Books, London.

Woodcock, George, 1947, *The Basis of Communal Living*, Freedom Press, London.

Woodcock, George, 1982, *Letter to the Past: An Autobiography*, Fitzhenry and Whiteside, Toronto.

Worpole, Ken and Orton, Jason, 2013, *The New English Landscape*, Field Station, London.

Worpole, Ken, 2015, *New Jerusalem: The Good City and the Good Society*, Swedenborg Society, London.

Worthen, John, 2006, *D.H. Lawrence: The Life of an Outsider*, Penguin, London.

ESSAYS

Berry, Neil, 2017, 'Pacifism's Führer: Dick Sheppard's Struggle to Avert World War', *Times Literary Supplement*, 1 December.

Berry, Neil, 2020, 'We Believe in Life: The Contentious Career of John Middleton Murry', *Times Literary Supplement*, 3 January.

Bevir, Mark and O'Brien, David, 2003, 'From Idealism to Communitarianism: The Inheritance and Legacy of John Macmurray', *History of Political Thought*, Vol. 24, No. 2, pp. 305–329.

Bostridge, Mark, 2017, 'Dick Sheppard's Pacifism', *Times Literary Supplement*, 8 December.

Churchill, Nick, 2012, 'Viva Iford: Bournemouth's Radical Russian Printers', *Dorset Life*, September.

Davison-Pégon, Claire, 2011, 'Samuel Solomonovich Koteliansky and British Modernism', *Translation and Literature*, Vol. 20, No. 3, pp. 334–347.

Harrison, J.F.C., 1962, 'Review of Heavens Below', *Political Science Quarterly*, Vol. 77, No. 3 (September), pp. 442–444.

Hunt, E.H. and Pam, S.J., 2011, 'Agricultural Depression in England, 1873–96: Skills Transfer and the "Redeeming Scots"', *Agricultural History Review*, Vol. 59, No. 1, pp. 81–100.

Kimber, Gerri, 2014, 'The Night of the Zeppelin', *Times Literary Supplement*, 4 September.

Lambert, Phoebe, 2003, 'Armed Conflict: A Pacifist Experience and the Implications for Counselling', *The Journal of Critical Psychology, Counselling and Psychotherapy*, June.

Mellown, Muriel, 'One Woman's Way to Peace: The Development of Vera Brittain's Pacifism', *Frontiers: A Journal of Women Studies*, Vol. 8, No. 2, 001–6.

O'Connell, Marina, 2014, 'Land Settlements in East Anglia', *Managed Retreat* freesheet, Essex.

O'Sullivan, Noel, 1998, 'The Tragic Vision in the Political Philosophy of Nikolai Berdyaev (1874–1948)', *History of Political Thought*, Vol. 19, No. 1, pp. 79–99.

Ross, Michael, L., 1984, '"Carrying on the Human Heritage": From Lady Chatterley's Lover to Nineteen Eighty-Four', *The D.H. Lawrence Review*, Vol. 17, No. 1.

Walker, Andrew, 2020, 'The "Uncertainty of Our Climate": Mary Kelly and Rural Theatre', in *Rural Modernity in Britain*, edited by Kristin Bluemel and Michael McCluskey, Edinburgh University Press, Edinburgh.

Ward, Colin, 2012, 'A Century of Land Settlement in Essex', in *Talking Green*, Five Leaves, Nottingham.

Watson, Joe, 1959, 'A Good Workman and his Friends: Recollections of John Middleton Murry', *The London Magazine*, 6/5.

Watson, Joe, 1962, 'Retrospect-8: The Adelphi', *Ambit*, No. 14, pp. 21–23.

Whitworth, Michael, H., 'Enemies of Cant: The Athenaeum (1919–21) and The Adelphi (1923–48)', in *The Oxford Critical and Cultural History of Modernist Magazines, Volume I: Britain and Ireland 1880–1955*, edited by Peter Brooker and Andrew Thacker, Oxford University Press, Oxford.

Worpole, Ken, 2020, 'The Land Question: Some Disciples Go Back to the Land', *Times Literary Supplement*, 3 January.

Appendix

Prophets of the new world

From his base at Frating Hall Farm, Cambridge graduate and farmer Trevor Howard planned to teach a course for the Workers' Educational Association in the Colchester area called 'Prophets of the New World'. His daughter Katherine recalled: 'He suggested to my mother that they should put together a series of lectures on "Blake, Whitman, Tolstoy, Lawrence – Prophets of a New World" into which they would introduce their own "philosophy of Life, spiritually speaking".' This ambition brings to mind John Macmurray's call for encouraging new ways of thinking, for as he said in a talk for radio in 1949: 'Ever since 1919 I have felt that I was educated for a world in which I have never lived; and have had to live in a world for which I was never educated.'

Trevor's list went back to William Blake and Walt Whitman, but his own particular heroes, and those of other Frating members, were Leo Tolstoy and D.H. Lawrence, ever-present in his life and mind. The Frating experiment, like The Adelphi Centre before it, grew out of a distinctive political and religious culture associated with a range of thinkers and writers whose lives and writings intersected, some now sadly forgotten. Below are listed those whose names recur in Frating letters, writings, talks and memories.

S.L. Bensusan (1872–1958). English-born son of a Jewish feather merchant. Journalist, novelist and erudite chronicler of Essex rural life and dialect. Lived at Langham in Essex adjacent to The Adelphi Centre, where he befriended many members and visitors; his sister Esther was married to the painter Lucien Pissarro, who visited often and painted the Dedham landscape.

Nikolai Berdyaev (1874–1948). Russian-born Marxist turned Christian existentialist philosopher, and author of many books. Arrested and interrogated in 1920 by the much-feared Felix Djerzhinsky, head of Soviet Russia's Cheka, but survived and was then deported. His Christian socialist anti-totalitarianism was much admired by Joe Watson, George Orwell and Iris Murdoch.

Vera Brittain (1893–1970). Served as a nurse during the First World War in which her fiancé, brother and other close friends were killed, leading her to write the acclaimed memoir *Testament of Youth* (1933). An active feminist, socialist and pacifist, she was close to many in the Adelphi circle, both at Langham and Frating. Her daughter Shirley Williams (née Catlin) worked at Frating Hall Farm for six months before going on to become a well-known politician in the Labour Party and then the SDP and Liberal Democrats.

Martin Buber (1878–1965). Born in Vienna, died in Jerusalem, Jewish, secular philosopher who espoused a form of existentialism, allied to communitarian socialism, whose book *I and Thou* (1923) was widely read and admired throughout the world. Corresponded with Joe Watson and John Macmurray.

Samuel Koteliansky (1880–1955). Translator who played a key role in bringing Russian literature to the English-speaking world in the first decades of the twentieth century, and who enjoyed close working relationships with Virginia Woolf, D.H. Lawrence, Mark Gertler and John Middleton Murry: now seen to have played a major role in the development of a modernist aesthetic that was 'ultimately to alter the literary landscape', according to critic Claire Davison-Pégon.

D.H. Lawrence (1885–1930). Pre-eminent novelist, poet, playwright and essayist of the early twentieth century; the imaginative vitalism inherent in his fiction and poetry inspired readers across the world. Famously and sometimes notoriously author of *Sons and Lovers* (1913), *Women in Love* (1920) and *Lady Chatterley's Lover* (1928), his travel writings, poetry, plays and letters have enthralled readers in recent times more so than the novels. Unequivocally one of the most influential writers of the twentieth century.

Frank Lea (1915–1977). Author of many books on literary history and religious aesthetics, a close friend of John Middleton Murry and Joe Watson, and regular visitor to Frating Hall Farm. His books include *Carlyle: Prophet of Today* (1943), *The Seed of the Church* (1948), *The Tragic Philosopher: A Study of Friedrich Nietzsche* (1957), *The Life of John Middleton Murry* (1960) and *The Ethics of Reason* (1975). A significant English writer and critic undeservedly forgotten today.

John Macmurray (1891–1976). Philosopher. Badly wounded in the First World War, awarded the Military Cross. Anglican who after the war controversially urged immediate reconciliation with Germany; he wrote on selfhood and the crucial importance of personal relations. In later years, he and his wife joined the Society of Friends. Rayner Heppenstall recorded that Macmurray 'dominated the 1936 summer school' at The Adelphi Centre. Friend and work colleague of Karl Polyani, and later of Theodor Adorno, he became a Quaker in later life.

John Middleton Murry (1889–1957). Founding editor of *The Adelphi* magazine, close friend of D.H. Lawrence, husband of Katherine Mansfield, prolific author of many books on literary matters, he is the central figure in the setting up of The Adelphi Centre in Langham, from which Frating Hall community developed. His success with *The Adelphi* magazine inspired Joe Watson and a number of other working-class readers to engage with literature and politics.

Iris Murdoch (1919–1999). Philosopher and novelist. Wrote a number of reviews for *The Adelphi* journal in 1943 and 1944, including 'Midnight Hour', 'Rebirth of Christianity' and 'Worship and the Common Life'. Admirer of Berdyaev and Simone Weil. Her 1958 novel *The Bell* describes a spiritual retreat with all its attendant problems, but with sympathy and insight. Trevor Howard thought the complexities of communal life imagined by Murdoch in that novel closely resembled those at Frating.

Reinhold Niebuhr (1892–1971). American left-wing pastor, described by Arthur Schlesinger as 'the most influential American theologian of the 20th century', Niebuhr played an important role in the civil rights movement, and though starting out a pacifist moved to a more pragmatic attitude to politics and power in later life. Lectured at the 1936 Adelphi summer school.

Max Plowman (1883–1941). A reluctant recruit in the First World War, badly injured in fighting, and during convalescence published a collection of poetry *A Lap Full of Seed*. Resigned his commission and was court-martialled for refusing to return to his unit, becoming a committed pacifist. Editorial member of *The Adelphi* from 1930, founding member of the Peace Pledge Union, co-founder with John Middleton Murry of The Adelphi Centre in 1934. Book reviewer, poet, friend of Orwell, at the centre of everything that happened at Langham.

Karl Polyani (1886–1964). Born into a German-speaking Jewish family in Hungary, Polyani moved to Vienna at the end of the First World War, where he converted to Protestantism. A social democrat and Christian thereafter, he moved to London in 1934 and became close to a number of influential Christian socialists in Britain and left-wing intellectuals including R.H. Tawney, G.D.H. Cole and John Macmurray. Famous for one major work on economics *The Great Transformation*, published in 1944. Lectured at the 1936 Adelphi summer school.

Richard Rees (1900–1970). Diplomat and painter, baronet, lecturer for the Workers' Educational Association, editor of *The Adelphi*, war hero, translator of the works of Simone

Weil, and author of *Brave Men: A Study of D H Lawrence and Simone Weil* (1958), *George Orwell: Fugitive from the Camp of Victory* (1961) and *Simone Weil: A Sketch for a Portrait* (1966). Took a keen interest in experiments at Langham and Frating.

Dick Sheppard (1880–1937). Anglican priest, Dean of Canterbury and charismatic Christian pacifist; founder of the Peace Pledge Union. Vera Brittain based the character of Robert Carbury in her novel *Born 1925* on Sheppard. Personal friend of Trevor and Enid Howard, Joe Watson and Phoebe Lambert's parents and other Frating members.

Leo Tolstoy (1828–1910). Born into a Russian aristocratic family, the writer gained international renown having published two of the greatest novels ever written, *War and Peace* in 1867 and *Anna Karenina* in 1877. In addition to those he wrote many other novels and short stories of great worth, but it was his espousal of a redemptive form of Christianity, including the ethic of non-violent resistance to arbitrary power that made him equally admired across the world. His ideas had a particular purchase in Britain where many of his pamphlets and religious teaching were translated and published for the first time.

Simone Weil (1909–1943). French philosopher and political activist with anarchist sympathies, born into a secular Jewish family, gravitating to a more Catholic mysticism, allied to a self-punishing asceticism in solidarity with human suffering, from which she ultimately died. Supporter of the Republican cause during the Spanish Civil War and the French resistance during the Second World War. Two key books were *Gravity and Grace* and *The Need for Roots*, the latter a foundational text for modern communitarianism. Subject of a biography *Simone Weil: A Sketch for a Portrait* by Richard Rees (see above), with introduction by John Middleton Murry.

Acknowledgements

I would like to thank the following for their help during the difficult period (for everybody) in which this book was written, whether they were conscious of helping or not: Jeff Barrett, Anthony Cartwright, Michael Chaplin, Ian Christie, John Christie, Gillian Darley, Nick Darton, Travis Elborough, Gareth Evans, Peter Evans, Bob Gilbert, Lisa Gormley, Victor Gray, Nick Groom, Angela Hammond, Dieter Helm, Richard Hill, Tanis Hinchcliffe, David Hodgson, Tobias Jones, Gerri Kimber, Adrian May, Jason Orton, Ruth Philo, Ali Pretty, Jules Pretty, Andrew Ray, Tamara Stoll, Richard Wentworth and Stephen Witherford, along with our steadfast friends and neighbours at Clissold Court, which during the pandemic was a hive of mutual aid and solidarity as always.

Special thanks are owed to Ros Green, Director of the Essex Book Festival, where the seeds of this book were first sown, to Marina O'Connell for her depth of knowledge of the Land Settlement Association, as well as early sight of her own book on sustainable farming, to Neil Berry for much invaluable advice and insight into the Lawrence–Murry relationship, and to Hayley Dixon and Joe Hill and everybody else at Focal Point Gallery for their magnificent 2016 exhibition on 'Radical Essex', and the extensive programme of walks, talks, tours and festivities which followed.

It was my old friend Dave Morley who was the first to read and comment on an early draft, and gave me much helpful advice, for which I am especially grateful. Having been an admirer of Little Toller Books for some time, I was delighted when publishers Adrian and Gracie Cooper responded so enthusiastically to the book proposal and promptly commissioned it, so special thanks to them too, and to Graham Shackleton and Jon Woolcott for also helping bring the book to fruition. To my brother Ian Worpole, lifetime thanks for sharing the good times and the bad times, and on this occasion, for drawing the maps. Finally, to my wife Larraine – thanks for everything

K.W.
2021, London

Little Toller Books

FORD, PINEAPPLE LANE, DORSET
W. littletoller.co.uk E. books@littletoller.co.uk

THROUGH THE WOODS *H. E. Bates*
MEN AND THE FIELDS *Adrian Bell*
HAVERGEY *John Burnside*
ORISON FOR A CURLEW *Horatio Clare*
SOMETHING OF HIS ART: WALKING WITH J. S. BACH *Horatio Clare*
ARBOREAL: WOODLAND WORDS *Adrian Cooper*
ISLAND YEARS, ISLAND FARM *Frank Fraser Darling*
LANDFILL *Tim Dee*
HERBACEOUS *Paul Evans*
THE SCREAMING SKIES *Charles Foster*
THE TREE *John Fowles*
AN ENGLISH FARMHOUSE *Geoffrey Grigson*
TIME AND PLACE *Alexandra Harris*
THE MAKING OF THE ENGLISH LANDSCAPE *W. G. Hoskins*
FOUR HEDGES *Clare Leighton*
DREAM ISLAND *R. M. Lockley*
EMPERORS, ADMIRALS AND CHIMNEY SWEEPERS *Peter Marren*
THE UNOFFICIAL COUNTRYSIDE *Richard Mabey*
RING OF BRIGHT WATER *Gavin Maxwell*
DIARY OF A YOUNG NATURALIST *Dara McAnulty*
WHERE? *Simon Moreton*
SEA STORY *Louisa Adjoa Parker*
LOVE, MADNESS, FISHING *Dexter Petley*
THE LONG FIELD *Pamela Petro*
SHALIMAR *Davina Quinlivan*
THE ASH TREE *Oliver Rackham*
ANCIENT WOODS OF THE HELFORD RIVER *Oliver Rackham*
LIMESTONE COUNTRY *Fiona Sampson*
MY HOUSE OF SKY: THE LIFE OF J. A. BAKER *Hetty Saunders*
SNOW *Marcus Sedgwick*
WATER AND SKY, RIDGE AND FURROW *Neil Sentance*
BLACK APPLES OF GOWER *Iain Sinclair*
BEYOND THE FELL WALL *Richard Skelton*
CORNERSTONES: SUBTERRANEAN WRITING *Mark Smalley*
IN PURSUIT OF SPRING *Edward Thomas*
ON SILBURY HILL *Adam Thorpe*
THE NATURAL HISTORY OF SELBORNE *Gilbert White*
NO MATTER HOW MANY SKIES HAVE FALLEN *Ken Worpole*
GHOST TOWN: A LIVERPOOL SHADOWPLAY *Jeff Young*